C000083750

PRACTICAL

Exercises in English

BY

HUBER GRAY BUEHLER

MASTER IN ENGLISH IN THE HOTCHKISS SCHOOL

ARRANGED FOR USE WITH

ADAMS SHERMAN HILL'S

"FOUNDATIONS OF RHETORIC"

NEW YORK

HARPER & BROTHERS PUBLISHERS

1895

Educ T 768.95.245

HARVARD COLLEGE LIBRARY
FROM THE ESTATE OF
EDWIN HALE ABBOT
DECEMBER 28, 1931

Copyright, 1895, by HARPER & BROTHERS.

All rights reserved.

This scarce antiquarian book is included in our special *Legacy Reprint Series*. In the interest of creating a more extensive selection of rare historical book reprints, we have chosen to reproduce this title even though it may possibly have occasional imperfections such as missing and blurred pages, missing text, poor pictures, markings, dark backgrounds and other reproduction issues beyond our control. Because this work is culturally important, we have made it available as a part of our commitment to protecting, preserving and promoting the world's literature. Thank you for your understanding.

PREFACE

THE art of using one's native tongue correctly and forcibly is acquired for the most part through imitation and practice, and is not so much a matter of knowledge as of habit. As regards English, then, the first duty of our schools is to set before pupils excellent models, and, in all departments of school-work, to keep a watchful eye on the innumerable acts of expression, oral and written, which go to form habit. Since, however, pupils come to school with many of their habits of expression already formed on bad models, our schools must give some attention to the special work of pointing out common errors of speech, and of leading pupils to convert knowledge of these errors into new and correct habits of expression. This is the branch of English teaching in which this little book hopes to be useful.

All the "Exercises in English" with which I am acquainted consist chiefly of "sentences to be corrected." To such exercises there are grave objections. If, on the one hand, the fault in the given sentence is not seen at a glance, the pupil is likely, as experience has shown, to pass it by and to change something that is not wrong. If, on

the other hand, the fault is obvious, the exercise has no
value in the formation of habit. Take, for example, two
"sentences for correction" which I select at random from
one of the most widely used books of its class: "I knew it
was him," and "Sit the plates on the table." A pupil of
any wit will at once see that the mistakes must be in
"him" and "sit," and knowing that the alternatives are
"he" and "set," he will at once correct the sentences
without knowing, perhaps, why one form is wrong, the
other right. He has not gained anything valuable; he has
simply "slid" through his exercise. Moreover, such "sentences for correction" violate a fundamental principle of
teaching English by setting before the impressionable
minds of pupils bad models. Finally, such exercises are
unnatural, because the habit which we hope to form in
our pupils is not the habit of correcting mistakes, but
the habit of avoiding them.

Correct English is largely a matter of correct choice between two or more forms of expression, and in this book
an attempt has been made, as a glance at the pages will
show, to throw the exercises, whenever possible, into a form
consistent with this truth. Though a pupil may *change*
"who" to "whom" without knowing why, he cannot
repeatedly *choose* correctly between these forms without
strengthening his own habit of correct expression.

This book has been prepared primarily as a companion
to Professor A. S. Hill's "Foundations of Rhetoric," in
answer to the request of many teachers for exercises to

use with that admirable work.[1] Without the friendly en-
couragement of Professor Hill the task would not have
been undertaken, and to him above all others I am indebted
for assistance in completing it. He has permitted me to
draw freely on his published works ; he has provided me
with advance sheets of the revised edition of " Principles
of Rhetoric ;" he has put at my disposal much useful material gleaned from his own experience ; he has read the
manuscript and proofs, and, without assuming any responsibility for shortcomings, he has suggested many improve-
ments. I am also indebted to Mr. E. G. Coy, Headmaster
of the Hotchkiss School, for many valuable suggestions,
and to my colleague, Mr. J. E. Barss, for assistance in the
proof-reading.

The quotations from " The Century Dictionary " are made
under an arrangement with the owners of the copyright
of that work. I am also indebted to Professor Barrett
Wendell, Messrs. Houghton, Mifflin & Co., and Messrs.
Macmillan & Co. for permission to use brief quotations
from their works.

H. G. B.

Lakeville, Conn., *September*, 1895.

---

[1] See Appendix: Suggestions to Teachers.

CONTENTS

PRACTICAL EXERCISES IN ENGLISH

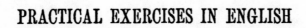

PRACTICAL
EXERCISES IN ENGLISH

CHAPTER I.

OF GOOD USE

WHY is it that for the purposes of English composition one word is not so good as another? To this question we shall get a general answer if we examine the effect of certain classes of expressions.

Present Use.—Let us examine first the effect produced by three passages in the authorized version of the English Bible—a version made by order of King James in 1611:—

"For these two years hath the famine been in the land: and yet there are five years, in the which there shall neither be *earing* nor harvest" (Gen. xlv. 6).

"O ye sons of men, how long will ye turn my glory into shame? how long will ye love vanity, and seek after *leasing?*" (Psa. iv. 2).

"Now I would not have you ignorant, brethren, that oftentimes I purposed to come unto you, but was *let* hitherto" (Rom. i. 13).

See also Gen. xxv. 29; Matt. iii. 8; Acts viii. 3; 1 Thess. iv. 15.

An ordinary reader of our time cannot without assistance fully understand these passages, because the words "earing," "leasing," and "let" convey to his mind either no idea at all or a wrong idea. Two hundred and eighty years ago, when this translation of the Bible was made, these words were common words with plain meanings; but "earing" and "leasing" have since dropped out of common use, and "let" has acquired a different meaning; consequently an ordinary reader of the present time must consult a dictionary before he can be sure what the passages mean. Words and meanings which have gone out of use are called *obsolete*. There is not much temptation to use obsolete words; but the temptation sometimes comes. Therefore we note, as our first conclusion, that a person who wishes to be understood must avoid expressions and meanings which are not in *present use*.

National Use.—A boy from southern Pennsylvania was visiting in New York State. In the midst of some preparations for a fishing excursion he said to his host, "Shall I take my *gums* along?" His host burst out laughing and said, "Of course; did you think of taking them out of your mouth and leaving them at home?"[1] Unconsciously the boy had used a good English word in a sense peculiar to the district in which he lived; his host had understood the word in its proper sense.

On another occasion a gentleman who had just arrived at a hotel in Kennebunkport, Me., agreed to a proposal to "go down to the beach in the *barge*." Going to his room, he prepared for a little excursion on the river which flowed by the hotel. When he returned, he was greatly surprised to find his friends about to start for the beach in *a large omnibus*. Another gentleman once asked a young lady to go "*riding*" with him. At the appointed hour he drove to her house in a buggy, and she came down to meet him in her riding habit.

These incidents show that if we use expressions that

---

[1] This and the two following incidents are from the writer's own observation.

are only local, or use words in local senses, we are liable either to be misunderstood or not to be understood at all. Obscurity also arises from the use of words in senses which are peculiar to a certain class or profession. For example, to a person who is not familiar with commercial slang, this sentence from the market columns of a newspaper is a puzzle:—

"Java coffees are *dull* and *easy*, though they are *statistically strong*."

The following directions for anchoring in a gale of wind are taken from a book called "How to Sail a Boat":—

"When everything is ready, bring the yacht *to the wind*, and let the sails shake *in the wind's eye;* and, so soon as she gets *stern-way*, let go the *best bower* anchor, taking care not to *snub her* too quickly, but to let considerable of the cable run out before checking her; then take a turn or two around the *knight-heads*," etc.

If a landsman's safety depended on his understanding these directions, there would not be much hope for him.

The following extract is from a newspaper report of a game of ball:—

"In the eighth inning Anson jumped from one box into the other and whacked a wide one into extreme right. It was a three-base jolt and was made when Gastright intended to force the old man to first. The Brooklyns howled and claimed that Anson was out, but McQuaid thought differently. Both teams were crippled. Lange will be laid up for a week or so. One pitcher was batted out of the box."

This narrative may seem commonplace to school-boys, but to their mothers and sisters it must seem alarming.

Our second conclusion, therefore, is that a person who wishes to be understood must avoid words and phrases that are not understood, and understood in the same sense, in every part of the country, and in every class or profession.[1]

Reputable Use.—Let us examine now the effect produced by a third kind of expression, namely, words and phrases "not used by writers and speakers of established reputation."[2] Let us take as our illustrations the familiar expressions, "He *done* it" and "Please *set* in this seat." Each of these expressions is common at the present time, and its meaning is instantly clear to any one who speaks English. But these expressions, not being used by well-informed and careful speakers, produce in the mind of a well-informed hearer an impression of vulgarity like that which we get from seeing a person eat with his knife. In language, as in manners and fashions, the law is found in the custom of the best people; and persons who wish to be classed as cultivated people must speak and write like cultivated people. There is no moral wrong in a person's saying "Please *set* in this seat," and if he does say it he will probably be understood; but persons who use this or any other expression which is not in reputable use run the risk of being classed as ignorant, affected, or vulgar.

Good Use.—It appears, therefore, that words and phrases, in order to be proper expressions for use in English prose, (1) must be in common use at the present time; (2) they must be used, and used in the same sense, in every part of the country, and in every class and profession; (3) they must be expressions used by writers and speakers of established reputation. In other words, our expressions must be in *present, national,* and *reputable* use. Expressions which fulfil these three conditions are said to be in *good use.*

The next question that presents itself to one who wishes

---

[1] A. S. Hill: Foundations of Rhetoric, p. 28.
[2] Ibid., p. 20.

to use English correctly is, How am I to know what words and expressions are in good use?

Conversation and Good Use.—Good use cannot be determined solely by observing the conversation of our associates; for the chances are that they use many local expressions, some slang, and possibly some vulgarisms. "You often hear it" is not proof that an expression is in good use.

Newspapers and Good Use.—Nor can good use be learned from what we see in newspapers. Newspapers of high rank contain from time to time, especially in their editorial columns, some of the best modern prose, and much literature that has become standard was first printed in periodicals; but most of the prose in newspapers is written necessarily by contributors who do not belong to the class of "speakers or writers whom the world deems the best." As the newspaper in its news records the life of every day, so in its style it too frequently records the slang of daily life and the faults of ordinary conversation. A newspaper contains bits of English prose from hundreds of different pens, some skilled, some unskilled; and this jumble of styles does not determine good use.

No one Book or Writer Decisive.—Nor is good use to be learned from our favorite author, unsupported by other authority; not even, as we have seen, from the English Bible, when it stands alone. No writer, even the greatest, is free from occasional errors; but these accidental slips are not to be considered in determining good use. Good use is decided by the prevailing usage of the writers whose works make up permanent English literature, not by their inadvertencies. "The fact that Shakspere uses a word, or Sir Walter Scott, or Burke, or Washington Irving, or whoever happens to be writing earnestly in Melbourne or Sidney, does not make it reputable. The fact that all five of

these authorities use the word in the same sense would go
very far to establish the usage.   On the other hand, the
fact that any number of newspaper reporters agree in
usage does not make the usage reputable.   The style of
newspaper reporters is not without merit; it is very rarely
unreadable; but for all its virtue it is rarely a well of English undefiled." [1]

"Reputable use is fixed, not by the practice of those
whom A or B deems the best speakers or writers, but by
the practice of those whom the world deems the-best,—
those who are in the best repute, not indeed as to thought,
but as to expression, the manner of communicating thought.
The practice of no one writer, however high he may stand
in the public estimation, is enough to settle a point; but
the uniform or nearly uniform practice of reputable speakers or writers is decisive." [2]

**Good Reading the Foundation of Good Speaking and
Writing.**—To the question how to become familiar with
good use the first answer is, read the best literature.
Language, like manners, is learned for the most part by
imitation; and a person who is familiar with the language
of reputable writers and speakers will use good English
without conscious effort, just as a child brought up among
refined people generally has good manners without knowing it.   Good reading is indispensable to good speaking or
writing.   Without this, rules and dictionaries are of no
avail.   In reading the biographies of eminent writers, it is
interesting to note how many of them were great readers
when they were young; and teachers can testify that
the best writers among their pupils are those who have
read good literature or who have been accustomed to
hear good English at home.   The student of expression

[1] Barrett Wendell: English Composition, p. 21.
[2] A. S. Hill: Principles of Rhetoric, revised edition, p. 16.

should begin at once to make the acquaintance of good literature.

The Use of Dictionaries.—To become acquainted with good literature, however, takes a long time; and to decide, by direct reference to the usage of the best writers, every question that arises in composition, is not possible for beginners. In certain cases beginners must go to dictionaries to learn what good use approves. Dictionaries do not make good use, but by recording the facts learned by professional investigators they answer many questions regarding it. To one who wishes to speak and write well a good dictionary is indispensable.

"The Foundations of Rhetoric."—Dictionaries, however, are not always a sufficient guide; for, being records, they aim to give *all* the senses in which a word is used, and do not always tell which sense is approved by the best usage. Large dictionaries contain many words which have gone out of good use and other words which have not yet come into good use. Moreover, they treat of words only, not of constructions and long expressions. Additional help in determining good use is required by beginners, and this help is to be found in such books as Professor A. S. Hill's "Foundations of Rhetoric." The investigations of a specialist are there recorded in a convenient form, with particular reference to the needs of beginners and of those who have been under the influence of bad models. Common errors are explained and corrected, and the fundamental merits of good expression are set forth and illustrated.

Purpose of these Exercises.—In the following exercises, which are intended for drill on some of these elements of good expression, care has been taken to. put the questions into the forms in which they arise in actual composition. The notes which precede the exercises are only hints; for

1*

full discussions of the principles involved the student must consult larger works.

Some Convenient Names

BARBARISMS: Words and phrases not English; *i.e.,* not authorized by good English use. The name comes from a Greek word meaning "foreign," "strange."

Phrases that have gone out of use, said to be ARCHAIC or OBSOLETE.

Brand-new words which have not become established in good use: as, "burglarize," "enthuse," "electrocute."

Phrases introduced from foreign countries (called FOREIGNISMS, ALIENISMS), or peculiar to some district or province (called PROVINCIALISMS). A phrase introduced from France is called a *Gallicism;* from England, an *Anglicism.* A phrase peculiar to America is called an *Americanism.* Similarly we have the terms *Latinism, Hellenism, Teutonism,* etc. All these names may be applied also to certain kinds of Improprieties and Solecisms.

IMPROPRIETIES: Good English words or phrases used in wrong senses: as, "I *guess* I'll go to bed;" "He is *stopping* for a week at the Berkshire Inn."

Most errors in the use of English are Improprieties, which are far more common than Barbarisms and Solecisms. No classification of them is here attempted.

SOLECISMS: Constructions not English, commonly called cases of "bad grammar" or "false syntax": as, "She invited Mrs. Roe and *I* to go driving with her." "Solecism" is derived from *Soli,* the name of a Greek tribe who lived in Cilicia and spoke bad Greek.

SLANG is a general name for current, vulgar, unauthorized language. It may take the form of barbarism, impropriety, or solecism.

A COLLOQUIALISM is an expression peculiar to familiar conversation.

A VULGARISM is an expression peculiar to vulgar or ignorant people.

EXERCISE I.

1. Make a list of the provincial expressions you can think of, and give their equivalents in national English.

2. Make a list of the slang or vulgar expressions you can think of, and give their equivalents in reputable English.

3. Make a list of the words, forms, and phrases not in present use which you can find in the second chapter of the Gospel of Matthew, authorized version, and give their equivalents in modern English.

EXERCISE II.

Which word in the following pairs should an American prefer? Consult Hill's "Foundations of Rhetoric," pp. 28–29: Coal, coals; jug, pitcher; street railway, tramway; post-card, postal-card; depôt, station.

EXERCISE III.

1. Arrange the following words in two columns, putting in the first column words that are in good use, in the second, words that are not in good use. Consult Hill's "Foundations of Rhetoric," pp. 27–29: Omnibus, succotash, welkin, ere, née, depôt, veto, function (in the sense of social entertainment), to pan out, twain, on the docket, kine, gerrymander, carven, caucus, steed, to coast (on sled or bicycle), posted (informed), to watch out, right (very).

2. Give good English equivalents for the words which are not in good use.

CHAPTER II.

OF ARTICLES

A or An.[1]—The choice between these forms is determined by sound, not by spelling. Before a consonant sound "a" is used; before a vowel sound "an" is used.

EXERCISE IV.

Put the proper form, "a" or "an," before each of these expressions:—Elephant, apple, egg, union of states, uniform, uninformed person, universal custom, umpire, Unitarian church, anthem, unfortunate man, united people, American, European, Englishman, one, high hill, horse, honorable career, hypocrite, humble spirit, honest boy, hypothesis, history, historical sketch, heir, hundred, hereditary disease, household.

The or A.[2]—"The" is a broken-down form of the old English *thæt*, from which we also get "that," and is used to point out some particular person, thing, or class: as, "*The* headmaster of *the* school gave *the* boys permission." When "the" is used before the name of a particular class of persons or things it is called the "generic" article (from *genus*, "a class"): as, "None but *the* brave deserve *the* fair"; "*The* eagle is our national bird."

"An" ("a") is a broken-down form of the old English word *ane*, meaning "one." It is properly used when the object is thought of as one of a class: as, "There is *an* eagle in the zoological garden." It cannot properly be used before a word which is used as a class name, because a class name includes in its meaning more than "one."

[1] "Foundations," pp. 32–33.
[2] Ibid., pp. 33–34.

Superfluous and **Omitted Articles.**¹—The use of a superfluous "a" or "an" before a class name, especially after
the words "sort" and "kind," is a common and obstinate
error. We may say, "This is an eagle," meaning "one
eagle." But we may not say, "*An* eagle is our national
bird," "This is a rare kind of *an* eagle," or, "It is not
worthy of the name of *an* eagle"; because in these sentences "eagle" is used as the name, not of a single bird, but
of a class of birds, and includes in its meaning all the birds
which belong to the class called "eagle." The sentences
are equivalent to: "The kind of bird called 'eagle' is our
national bird;" "This is a rare species of the class of birds
called 'eagle;'" "It is not worthy of the name given to the
birds which belong to the class called 'eagle.'"

EXERCISE V.

Tell the difference in meaning between :—

1. The (a) house is on fire.
2. Yes, I heard (the) shouts in the street.
3. About eight o'clock (the) guests began to come.
4. Yes, I heard (the) noises in the next room.
5. The (an) elephant stood on a cask, and the (a) clown sat on the elephant's back.
6. The President has appointed a commission to investigate the cause of (the) strikes.
7. Will he let us look at (the) stars through the (a) telescope?
8. (The) teacher and (the) pupil are interested in this question.
9. He told us about an (the) accident.
10. Fire is beautiful. The fire is beautiful.
11. He was a better scholar than (an) athlete.
12. A young and (a) delicate girl.
13. He liked the bread and (the) butter.
14. A pink and (a) lavender gown.
15. The wise and (the) good.
16. Wanted, a cook and (a) housemaid.
17. The black and (the) white cow.

¹ "Foundations," pp. 34–39.

18. The athlete, (the) soldier, (the) statesman, and (the) poet.

19. A secretary and (a) treasurer.

20. The corresponding and (the) recording secretary.

21. The honest, (the) wise, and (the) patriotic senators voted against the bill.

22. A cotton and (a) silk umbrella.

23. The tenth and (the) last chapter.

EXERCISE VI.

Insert the proper article ("a," "an," or "the") in each blank place in the following, if an article is needed; if no article is needed, leave the place blank:—

1. I began to suffer from — want of food.

2. There are two articles, the definite and — indefinite.

3. He did not say what kind of — horse he wanted to buy.

4. Did Macaulay die of — heart disease?

5. Nouns have two numbers, — singular and — plural.

6. — third and — fourth page are to be learned.

7. — third and — fourth pages are to be learned.

8. Many names of — states are derived from — Indian tongues.

9. This is a curious species of — rose.

10. Study carefully — first and — second chapters.

11. A black and — white boy were walking together.

12. — violet is my favorite flower; — robin, my favorite bird.

13. There is an impenetrable veil between — visible and — invisible world.

14. — lion is — king of beasts.

15. Thackeray was a greater writer than — artist. Thackeray was greater as — writer than as — artist.

16. The bank closed its doors from — lack of ready money.

17. I despise not — giver, but — gift.

18. — whole is greater than any of its parts.

19. He is entitled to the name of — scholar.

20. I do not use that sort of — pen.

21. In — warm weather you do not need so many wraps as in — cold weather.

22. The Queen conferred on Tennyson the title of — baron.

23. It does not matter what kind of — man is appointed.

24. It is found in both — old and — new editions.

25. The fourth and — fifth verse.

26. The fourth and — fifth verses.

27. Franklin was — great and — good man.

28. — families of — strikers are sadly in — need of food.

29. Here are two bottles, — one empty, — other full of — red liquid.

30. Ariel had — power to control — sea.

31. Evangeline travelled far in — search of Gabriel.

32. Illustrate by an original sentence — preterite and — past participle of the following verbs.

33. To — student of Latin or Greek a knowledge of — difference in meaning in English between — indicative and — subjunctive is especially important.

34. In the verb "to be" — present and — past subjunctives have different forms.

35. — life in Madras in — time of Clive was different from what it is now.

36. I like so many sports that it is hard to tell which I like — best. I like swimming, foot-ball, and riding more than — others, but I do not know which of these three I like — best.

CHAPTER III.

OF NOUNS

How to Form the Possessive Case.[1]—As a rule, the possessive of nouns in the SINGULAR number is formed by adding an apostrophe and "s" ('s): as, "The *boy's* coat." Often the pronunciation of the added "s" makes a new syllable; and if this additional syllable makes an unpleasant sound, the possessive is indicated by the apostrophe alone ('): as, "For *goodness'* sake." The putting in or the leaving out of the "s" in such cases is chiefly a matter of taste. If the "s" is sounded, it is always written; and whenever there is doubt, it is well to follow the regular rule: as, "*Horace's* odes," "*Charles's* ball," "*Dickens's* David Copperfield."

In the PLURAL number, when the nominative plural ends in "s," the possessive case is formed by adding an apostrophe alone ('). If the nominative plural does not end in "s," an apostrophe and an "s" ('s) are both added, as in the singular: as, "*Men's* and *boys'* shoes."

The possessive case of COMPOUND nouns and expressions used as compound nouns is formed by adding the proper sign of the possessive to the end of the compound: as, "That is my *sister-in-law's* pony," "This is the *Prince of Wales's* palace."

EXERCISE VII.[2]

1. *Write the possessive case, singular and plural, of:* Actor, king, fairy, calf, child, goose, lady, monkey, mouse, ox, woman, deer, eagle, princess, elephant, man, witness, prince, fox, farmer, countess, mouth, horse, day, year, lion, wolf, thief, Englishman.

[1] "Foundations," pp. 41–43.
[2] TO THE TEACHER.—To have its full value this should be given as a dictation exercise.

2. *Write the possessive case of:* James, Dickens, his sister Mary, Miss Austen, the Prince of Wales, Frederick the Great, Harper and Brothers, father - in - law, Charles, Jones, William the Conqueror, Henry the Eighth, man-of-war, Douglas, Eggleston and Company.

Use and Misuse of the Possessive Case.[1]—It is sometimes a question whether to use the possessive form or the preposition *of.* "As a general rule, the possessive case should be confined to cases of possession."[2]

EXERCISE VIII.

Express relation between the words in the following pairs by putting one of them in the possessive case or by using the preposition "of," as may seem best:—

Charles the Second, reign; witness, testimony; horse, hoof; the President, public reception; Partridge, restaurant; aide - de - camp, horse; General Armistead, death; Henry the Eighth, wives; Napoleon, Berlin decree; teacher, advice; eagle, talons; enemy, repulse;[3] book, cover; princess, evening gowns; France, army; Napoleon, defeat; Napoleon, camp - chest; Major André, capture; Demosthenes, orations; gunpowder, invention; mountain, top; summer, end; Washington, sword; Franklin, staff; torrent, force; America, metropolis; city, streets; strike, beginning; church, spire; we (our, us), midst; year, events; Guiteau, trial; sea, bottom; Essex, death; Adams, administration; six months, wages; world, government.

EXERCISE IX.

Distinguish between the following:—

1. The President's reception. The reception of the President.
2. Mother's love. Love of mother.
3. A sister's care. Care of a sister.
4. A brother's picture. The picture of a brother.
5. Clive's reception in London. The reception of Clive in London.
6. Charles and Harry's toys. Charles's and Harry's toys.
7. Let me tell you a story of Doctor Brown (Brown's).

[1] "Foundations," pp. 43–44.

[2] Ibid., p. 44.

[3] There is, properly, no "objective possessive" in English corresponding to the "objective genitive" in other languages. It seems best to say "The siege of Paris," rather than "Paris's siege."

EXERCISE X.

Correct the following, giving the reason for each correction:—

1. A dog and a cat's head are differently shaped.
2. Whose Greek grammar do you prefer—Goodwin or Hadley?
3. It is neither the captain nor the manager's duty.
4. I consulted Webster, Stormonth, and Worcester's dictionary.
5. I like Hawthorne better than Irving's style.
6. John, Henry, and William's nose resembled one another.
7. The novel is one of Scott.
8. I have no time to listen to either John or Joseph's talk.

Singular and Plural.[1]—In modern English most nouns form the plural by adding "s" to the singular. The following variations from this rule are important:—

1. When the added sound of "s" makes an additional syllable, "es" is used: as, box, boxes; church, churches.

2. **Nouns ending in "o."** If the final "o" is preceded by a vowel, the plural is formed regularly, *i.e.*, by adding "s": as, cameo, cameos. If the final "o" is preceded by a consonant, the tendency of modern usage is to form the plural by adding "es": as, hero, heroes; potato, potatoes. The following common words, however, seem still to form the plural by adding "s" alone:—

canto	lasso	proviso	torso
duodecimo	memento	quarto	tyro
halo	octavo	solo	
junto	piano	stiletto	

3. **Nouns ending in "y."** If the "y" is preceded by a vowel, the plural is regular: as, valley, valleys.

If the "y" is preceded by a consonant, "y" is changed to "i" and "es" is added to form the plural: as, lady, ladies; city, cities.

4. **Proper nouns** are changed as little as possible: as, Henry, Henrys; Mary, Marys; Cicero, Ciceros; Nero, Neros.

5. Most **compound nouns** form the plural by adding the proper sign of the plural to the fundamental part of the word, *i.e.*, to the part which is described by the rest of the phrase: as, ox-cart, ox-carts; court-martial, courts-martial; aide-de-camp, aides-de-camp.

Note the difference between the *plural* and the *possessive* of compound nouns,—forms which are often confounded. See page 16.

[1] "Foundations," pp. 45–47.

6. Letters, figures, and other **symbols** are made plural by adding an apostrophe and "**s**" ('**s**): as, "There are more *e's* than *a's* in this word"; "Dot your *i's* and cross your *t's*."

7. Some nouns have two plurals, which differ in meaning:—

Singular.	*Plural.*
brother	brothers (by birth), brethren (of a society).
die	dies (for coining or stamping), dice (for play).
fish	fishes (separate fish), fish (collective).
index	indexes (in books), indices (in algebra).
penny	pennies (separate coins), pence (sum of money).
shot	shots (discharges), shot (balls).
staff	staves (poles), staffs (bodies of assistants).

EXERCISE XI.[1]

Write the plural of: Lash, cage, race, buffalo, echo, canto, volcano, portfolio, ally, money, solo, memento, mosquito, bamboo, ditch, chimney, man, Norman,[2] Mussulman, city, negro, baby, calf, man-of-war, attorney, goose-quill, canon, quail, mystery, turkey, wife, body, snipe, knight-errant, donkey, spoonful, aide-de-camp, Ottoman, commander-in-chief, major-general, pony, reply, talisman, court-martial, father-in-law, court-yard, man-trap, Brahman, journey, Henry, stepson, deer, mouthful, Miss Clark,[3] Mr. Jones, Dr. Brown, Dutchman, German, forget-me-not, poet-laureate, minister-plenipotentiary, hero, fish, trout, Mary, George, bill-of-fare.

EXERCISE XII.

Distinguish between:—

1. Two dice (dies) were found in the prisoner's pockets.
2. He was always kind to his brothers (brethren).
3. How many shot (shots) did you count?
4. He carried two pailfuls (pails full) of water up the hill.
5. I have two handfuls (hands full) of gold-dust.
6. He gave the beggar six pennies (pence).
7. There are serious errors in the indexes (indices) in this new Algebra.
8. Ten shot (shots) were fired from the gun in fifteen minutes.

---

[1] To the Teacher.—To have its full value this should be given as a dictation exercise. [2] Consult a dictionary for this and similar nouns.

[3] Proper names preceded by a title are made plural by changing either the name or the title, and using "the" before the expression. We may say "the Miss Smiths" or "the Misses Smith," "the Doctors Young" or "the Doctor Youngs."

EXERCISE XIII.

Which of the following forms should be used? Consult Hill's
"Foundations," pp. 45–47 :—

1. The members of the committee were greatly alarmed at this (these) news.

2. Tidings was (were) brought to them of the massacre on Snake River.

3. The endowment of the college was greatly increased by this (these) means.

4. The widow's means was (were) at first large, but it was (they were) soon exhausted by the prodigality of her son.

5. The assets of the company are (is) $167,000.

6. The dregs in the cup was (were) found to be very bitter.

7. The eaves of the new house are (is) thirty-two feet above the ground.

8. Athletics are (is) run into the ground in many schools.

9. Politics is (are) like a stone tied around the neck of literature.

10. The nuptials of Gratiano and Nerissa were (was) celebrated at the same time as those (that) of Bassanio and Portia.

11. Ethics are (is) becoming more and more prominent in the discussions of political economists.

12. Have you seen my pincers?   I have mislaid it (them).

13. The proceeds was (were) given to the hospital.

14. His riches took to themselves (itself) wings.

15. This (these) scissors is (are) not sharp.

16. Please pour this (these) suds on the rose plants in the oval flower-bed.

17. His tactics was (were) much criticised by old generals.

18. The United States has (have) informed Spain that it (they) will not permit Spanish interference in the affairs of Central America.

Nouns of Foreign Origin.[1]—The following is a list of nouns of foreign origin in common use which have peculiar number forms :—

Singular.	Plural.
alumnus (masculine)	alumni
alumna (feminine)	alumnæ
analysis	analyses
bacterium	bacteria

[1] "Foundations," pp. 47–48.

Singular.	Plural.
beau	beaux
cherub	cherubim (or cherubs)
crisis	crises
curriculum	curricula
datum	data
genus (meaning "class")	genera
genius	{ geniuses (persons of great ability) { genii (spirits)
hypothesis	hypotheses
oasis	oases
parenthesis	parentheses
phenomenon	phenomena
seraph	seraphim (or seraphs)
stratum	strata
tableau	tableaux
thesis	theses

EXERCISE XIV.[1]

1. *Write the plural of:* Alumna, analysis, beau, cherub, crisis, curriculum, genus, genius, hypothesis, nebula, oasis, parenthesis, phenomenon, synopsis, seraph, stratum, tableau.

2. *Write the singular of:* Alumni, curricula, data, bacteria, cherubim, oases, phenomena, seraphim, strata, theses.

Gender.—The following nouns of different genders are sometimes confounded or otherwise misused :—

Masculine.	Feminine.	Masculine.	Feminine.
abbot	abbess	gander	goose
actor	actress	hero	heroine
bachelor	spinster, maid	lion	lioness
buck	doe (fallow deer)	marquis, marquess	marchioness
bullock	heifer	monk	nun
czar	czarina	ram	ewe
drake	duck	stag, hart	hind (red deer)
duke	duchess	sultan	sultana
earl	countess	tiger	tigress
Francis	Frances	wizard	witch

[1] To THE TEACHER.—To have any value this must be given as a dictation exercise.

EXERCISE XV.[1]

1. *Write the feminine word corresponding to:* Abbot, actor, bachelor, buck, bullock, czar, duke, drake, earl, Francis, hero, lion, marquis, monk, ram, stag, sultan, hart, tiger.

2. *Write the masculine word corresponding to:* Spinster, duck, doe, Frances, goose, heifer, ewe, hind, witch.

EXERCISE XVI.

Correct the following sentences:—

1. The marquess was the executor of her husband's estate.
2. He married a beautiful actor.
3. The tiger broke from its cage.
4. The duck was pluming his feathers after his swim, and the goose had wandered from his companions across the meadows.
5. The baby girl in "The Princess" may be called the real hero of the tale.

Abbreviations.—For the following exercise consult Hill's Foundations of Rhetoric, pp. 49–50.

EXERCISE XVII.

Which of these words are in good use?—

Pianist, harpist, poloist, violinist, phiz, ad, co-ed, curios, exam, cab, chum, gent, hack, gym, pants, mob, phone, proxy, photo, prelim, van, prof, varsity.

Misused Nouns.[2]—Many errors in English consist in using words in senses which are not authorized. Sometimes the use of a word in a wrong sense makes the speaker's meaning obscure. Sometimes it makes him seem ridiculous, as when a person of the writer's acquaintance told a friend to clean an oil-painting by washing it in "torpid" water.

[1] To THE TEACHER.—This should be used as a dictation exercise.

[2] To THE TEACHER.—It may not be desirable to drill pupils on all the words whose meanings are discriminated here and in chapters V. and VI. In that case it will be easy to select for study those words which the pupils are most likely to misuse. The words discriminated in this book are for the most part those which are mentioned in the "Foundations of Rhetoric," and they have been arranged in the same order. A few other words often misused by my pupils have been added.

In every case the misuse of a word leaves an unpleasant impression on the mind of a cultivated person, and, like all bad English, should be avoided as we avoid bad manners. In the following definitions and exercises a few nouns[1] are selected for study. The distinctions given are not always observed by reputable authors, but they indicate the *tendency* of the best modern usage.

I. A RESEMBLANCE IN SENSE MISLEADS.[2]

House, home.—A *house* is a building. *Home* means one's habitual abode, "the abiding place of the affections." It may or may not be in a house, and it may include the surroundings of a house.

Person, party.—A *person* is an individual; a *party* is a company of persons, or, in legal usage, a person who is concerned in a contention or agreement.

Series, succession.—A *series* is a succession of similar things mutually related according to some law. *Succession* is properly used of several things following one after the other; it denotes order of occurrence only, and does not imply any connection.

Statement, assertion.—A *statement* is a formal setting forth of fact or opinion; an *assertion* is simply an affirmation of fact or opinion.

Verdict, testimony.—A *verdict* is a decision made by a number of men acting as a single body. *Testimony* is an expression of individual knowledge or belief.

The whole, all.—*The whole* is properly used of something which is considered as one thing. When a number of persons or things are spoken of, the proper word is *all*.

EXERCISE XVIII.

Tell the difference in meaning between the following:—

1. Mr. Roscoe has no house (home).
2. The hotel clerk says he expects three more parties (persons) on the six o'clock train.
3. There are three persons (parties) concerned in this contract.
4. A succession (series) of delays.

---

[1] For misused *verbs* and *adjectives* see pages 61 and 109.
[2] "Foundations," pp. 50–53.

5. This morning's papers publish an assertion (a statement) by Mr. Pullman, which throws new light on the strike.

EXERCISE XIX.

Insert the proper word in each blank, and give the reason for your choice:—

House, home.

1. Whenever a tramp comes to our —, the dog is untied.
2. His new — will be finished in November.
3. Mr. S. owns a beautiful — and has a happy —.
4. One can build a very good — for $6000.
5. —s are built to live in, not to look on.

Party, person.

6. There is another — coming on the evening train, but he will leave to-morrow.
7. A cross-looking — alighted from the stage-coach and entered the inn.
8. The cause of both —s shall come before the court.
9. Is the — that wants a carriage at dinner or in his room?
10. He is attached to the king's —.
11. Who was that fat old — who kept us all laughing?

Series, succession.

12. The — of Presidents is a long one.
13. This stamp belongs to the — of 1864.
14. A — of calamitous events followed this mistake in policy.
15. A — of accidents prevented the sailing of the yacht.

Statement, assertion.

16. The last — of the bank has been examined.
17. — unsupported by fact is worthless.
18. The Declaration of Independence contained a clear — of grievances.
19. The orator's — was shown to be false.

Verdict, testimony.

20. The — of history is that Christianity has improved the condition of women.
21. Let us await the — of the public.
22. The early Christian martyrs sealed their — with their blood.
23. The — of those who saw the murder was contradictory.

The whole, all.

24. — (of) the dishes came tumbling to the floor.

25. Tell — (the) truth.

26. Then you and I and — of us fell down.

27. Washington was respected by — (the) people.

28. We sold — (of) our apples at sixty cents a bushel.

29. He has already packed — of his books.

30. — (the) adornments took an appropriate and sylvan character.

31. He readily confided to her — (the) papers concerning the intrigue.

32. In the afternoon — of them got into a boat and rowed across the lake.

II. A RESEMBLANCE IN SOUND MISLEADS.[1]

Acceptance, acceptation.—*Acceptance* is the "act of accepting"; also "favorable reception": as, "The acceptance of a gift," "She sang with marked acceptance." *Acceptation* now means "the sense in which an expression is generally understood or accepted."

Access, accession.—*Access* has several meanings authorized by good use: (1) outburst; (2) admission; (8) way of entrance. *Accession* means (1) the coming into possession of a right; or (2) an addition.

Acts, actions.—"*Acts*, in the sense of 'things done,' is preferable to *actions*, since *actions* also means 'processes of doing.'"[2]

Advance, advancement.—*Advance* is used in speaking of something as moving forward ; *advancement*, as being moved forward.

Allusion, illusion, delusion.—An *allusion* is an indirect reference to something not definitely mentioned. Roughly speaking, an *illusion* is an error of vision; *delusion*, of judgment. "In literary and popular use an *illusion* is an unreal appearance presented in any way to the bodily or the mental vision ; it is often pleasing, harmless, or even useful. . . . A *delusion* is a mental error or deception, and may have regard to things actually existing, as well as to *illusions*. *Delusions* are ordinarily repulsive and discreditable, and may even be mischievous."[3]

Avocation, vocation.—"*Vocation* means 'calling' or 'profession'; *avocation*, 'something aside from one's regular calling, a by-work.'"[4]

---

[1] "Foundations," pp. 53–56.

[2] A. S. Hill: Principles of Rhetoric, revised edition, p. 18.

[3] The Century Dictionary.

[4] A. S. Hill: Principles of Rhetoric, revised edition, p. 39.

2

Completion, completeness.—*Completion* is "the act of completing"; *completeness* is "the state of being complete."

Observation, observance.—*Observation* contains the idea of "looking at"; *observance*, of "keeping," "celebrating." "We speak of the *observation* of a fact, of a star; of the *observance* of a festival, of a rule."[1]

Proposal, proposition.—"A *proposal* is something proposed to be done, which may be accepted or rejected. A *proposition* is something proposed for discussion, with a view to determining the truth or wisdom of it."[2]

Relationship, relation.—*Relationship* properly means "the state of being related by kindred or alliance": as, "A relationship existed between the two families." *Relation* is a word of much broader meaning. It does not necessarily imply kinship.

Solicitude, solicitation.—*Solicitude* is "anxiety"; *solicitation* is "the act of soliciting or earnestly asking."

Stimulation, stimulus, stimulant.—*Stimulation* is "the act of stimulating or inciting to action"; *stimulus*, originally "a goad," now denotes that which stimulates, the means by which one is incited to action; *stimulant* has a medical sense, being used of that which stimulates the body or any of its organs. We speak of ambition as a *stimulus*, of alcohol as a *stimulant*.

EXERCISE XX.

Tell the difference in meaning between—

1. The acceptance (acceptation) of this word is doubtful.
2. The acts (actions) of Napoleon were carefully observed.
3. The colonel's advance (advancement) was not long delayed.
4. Literature has been Dr. Holmes's avocation (vocation).
5. The list of African dialects is approaching completeness (completion).
6. The completion (completeness) of this new dictionary of the Latin language will make scholars glad.
7. The professor advised me, when I went to Rome, to be especially careful in my observation (observance) of the religious ceremonies of Passion Week.
8. This proposal (proposition) of the Populist senator made both Republican and Democratic senators indignant.

[1] A. S. Hill: Principles of Rhetoric, revised edition, p. 39.
[2] The Century Dictionary.

9. His mother's solicitude (solicitation) induced Washington when he was a boy to give up his intention of going to sea.

10. Shall I give your son a stimulus (stimulant)?

EXERCISE XXL

Insert the proper word in each blank, and give the reason for your choice:—

Acceptance, acceptation.

1. The word "livery" is used in its original —.
2. This is a true saying and worthy of —.
3. The — of a trust brings grave responsibility.
4. He sent to the President a formal — of the position.
5. The assertion finds — in every rank of society.
6. In its common — "philosophy" signifies "the search after wisdom."
7. The probability of this theory justifies its full —.

Access, accession.

8. We are denied — to the king.
9. An — of fever occurred at nightfall.
10. The emperor at his — takes an oath to maintain the constitution.
11. — to the outer court was through a massive door.
12. The only — which the Roman Empire received was the province of Britain.
13. A sudden — of violent, burning fever had laid Peter's mother-in-law prostrate.
14. Victoria married after her — to the throne.
15. This allusion led to a fresh — of feeling.

Act, action.

16. I cannot do so cruel an —.
17. Another mode of — was proposed by him.
18. The fifth book of the New Testament records the —s of the Apostles.
19. To attempt resistance would be the — of a madman.
20. The monkey imitates the —s of its master.

Advance, advancement.

21. The — of the expedition was impeded by bad roads.
22. — in the army is slow.

23. The Don and his companions, in their eager —, had got entangled in deep glens.

24. My old position offered no hope of —.

25. His hopes of — in England failing, Swift returned to Ireland.

Allusion, illusion, delusion.

26. There were two —s in his sermon to the riots.

27. The cleverest, acutest men are often under an (a) — about women.

28. Longfellow's "Footsteps of Angels" contains —s to the death of his wife.

29. Our judgment of people is liable to be warped by —s of the imagination.

30. Those other words of — and folly, Liberty first and Union afterward.

Avocation, vocation.

31. Surgeons in the army are allowed by the enemy to pursue their — unmolested.

32. The young lawyer, surrounded by his law-books, took up his — with enthusiasm.

33. Let your base-ball be a pastime, not a trade; let it be your —, not your —.

34. Heaven is a pious man's —, and therefore he counts earthly employments —s.

35. It seems that after his return, his disciples left him and returned to their ordinary —s.

Completion, completeness.

36. The — of the railroad was celebrated by a general illumination in the village.

37. The comfort of passengers is secured by the — of the equipment of the steamers of this line.

38. We hope for the — of our new building by September.

39. We were surprised at the — of the collection of minerals.

Observation, observance.

40. The — of a few simple rules of health would have prolonged his life.

41. The North American Indian has great powers of —.

42. He insisted on the prompt — of the regulations.

43. The Pharisees were strict in their — of religious festivals.

44. He is arranging for a careful — of the eclipse.

Proposal, proposition.

45. I submit two —s for consideration by the assembly.

46. The — that each of us relinquish something was accepted.

47. Sealed —s for building the cottage were handed in by three contractors.

48. He made a — of marriage to her.

49. I dissent from that —.

50. A nation dedicated to the — that all men are created equal.

Solicitude, solicitation.

51. He made frequent — for money and clothes.

52. My mother watched over my infancy with tender —.

53. Coriolanus yielded at the — of his mother.

Stimulus, stimulant, stimulation.

54. He worked hard under the — of a desire to get rich.

55. The providential — of conscience is always present.

56. The doctor came and administered a gentle — to the patient.

III. ADDITIONAL NOUNS SOMETIMES MISUSED.[1]

Ability, capacity.—*Ability* is the power of doing; *capacity*, the power of containing, of understanding, of acquiring.

Adherence, adhesion.—*Adherence* is used of moral relations, *adhesion*, of physical connection. We speak of the *adhesion* of glue to wood, of a man's *adherence* to the principles of his party.

Amount, quantity, number.—*Amount* means "sum total," and is used of numbers or quantities; *quantity* is used of things which are measured; *number*, of things which are counted.

Argument, plea.—"*Plea* (in the legal sense) is properly used of the pleadings or the arraignment before a trial, not of the *argument* at a trial. A *plea* is always addressed to the court; an *argument* may be addressed either to the court or to the jury. A similar remark applies to the verbs *plead* and *argue*."[2]

Balance, rest, remainder.—*Balance*, meaning "the difference between two sides of an account," is a commercial term, and cannot properly be used for *rest* or *remainder*. *Rest* is used of persons or

---

[1] "Foundations," p. 56. If it seem undesirable to drill pupils on all the words which are here discriminated, the teacher may select those words which they are most likely to misuse. See note 2, p. 22.

[2] A. S. Hill: Principles of Rhetoric, revised edition, p. 40.

things, and of large as well as of small parts. *Remainder* is used only of things, and denotes a comparatively small part.

Centre, middle.—The *centre* is a point, or a definite place; the *middle* is a line, or a space, and is less definite than *centre*.

Character, reputation.—*Character* is what a man is; *reputation* is the prevailing opinion of his character.

Complement, compliment.—A *complement* is a "full quantity or number" or "that which is needed to complete"; a *compliment* is "an expression of praise."

Conscience, consciousness.—*Conscience* is that within us which distinguishes right from wrong. *Consciousness* is the state of being aware of one's existence, thoughts, and surroundings.

Council, counsel.—A *council* is "a body of persons convened for consultation." *Counsel* denotes "advice," or "a person, as a lawyer, engaged to give advice."

Custom, habit.—*Custom* denotes the frequent repetition of the same act, and may be used of a number of persons taken together. *Habit* is the effect of custom in a person. *Custom* is voluntary; *habit* is involuntary, often uncontrollable, sometimes unconscious.

Deception, deceit.—*Deception* is "the act of deceiving"; *deceit* is "deceitfulness," a trait of character; or a "trick," an "artifice."

Egoists, egoism, egotism.—"The disciples of Descartes were *egoists*, the *ego* being the basis of their philosophy." *Egoism* is the name of their system. *Egoism* is sometimes used also in the sense of undue admiration of self, the outward expression of which is *egotism*. But "*egotism*, in the sense of 'self-worship,' is preferable to *egoism*, since *egoism* also designates a system of philosophy." [1]

Emigration, immigration.—*Emigration* is the moving out from a country; *immigration*, the moving into it. Foreigners who come to live in America are *emigrants* from their fatherland, *immigrants* to America.

Enormity, enormousness.—"*Enormity* is used of deeds of unusual horror; *enormousness*, of things of unusual size. We speak of the *enormity* of Cæsar Borgia's crimes, of the *enormousness* of the Rothschilds' wealth." [2]

Esteem, estimate, estimation.—*Esteem* as a noun seems to be going out of use; the word now commonly used in the sense of "opinion"

[1] A. S. Hill: Principles of Rhetoric, revised edition, p. 19.
[2] Ibid., p. 38.

or "regard" is *estimation*. An *estimate* is "an approximate judgment, based on considerations of probability, of the number, amount, magnitude, or position of anything."

Falsity, falseness.—"*Falsity*, in the sense of 'non-conformity to truth,' without any suggestion of blame, is preferable to *falseness*, since *falseness* usually implies blame." [1]

Identity, identification.—*Identity* is "the state of being the same." *Identification* denotes "the act of determining what a given thing, or who a given person, is."

Import, importance.—*Import*, in the sense of "meaning," must be distinguished from *importance*, "the quality of being important."

Invent, discover.—We *invent* something new, contrived or produced for the first time. We *discover* what existed before, but remained unknown.

Limit, limitation.—*Limit*, in the sense of "bound," is preferable to *limitation*, since *limitation* also means "the act of limiting," or a "restriction."

Lot, number.—*Lot* denotes "a distinct part or parcel": as, "The auctioneer sold the goods in ten *lots*." The word does not mean "a great number"; therefore it is improperly used in the sentences: "He has *lots* of money," and "I know a *lot* of people in New York."

Majority, plurality.—A *majority* is more than half the whole number; a *plurality* is the excess of votes given for one candidate over those given for another, and is not necessarily a *majority* when there are more than two candidates.

Negligence, neglect.—"*Negligence* is used of a habit or trait; *neglect*, of an act or succession of acts." [2]

Novice, novitiate.—*Novice* properly means one who is new in any business or calling; *novitiate*, the state or time of being a *novice*.

Organism, organization.—An *organism* is a "living body composed of a number of essential parts." *Organization* denotes "the act of organizing," or "an organized body of persons," as a literary society.

Part, portion.—"*Part* is the general word for that which is less than the whole: as, the whole is equal to the sum of all its *parts*. . . . *Portion* is often used in a stilted way where *part* would be simpler and better; *portion* has always some suggestion of allotment or as-

---

[1] A. S. Hill: Principles of Rhetoric, revised edition, p. 19.
[2] Ibid., p. 39.

signment: as, this is my *portion;* a *portion* of Scripture. 'Father, give me the *portion* of goods that falleth to me.'" [1]

Plenty, abundance.—*Plenty* is enough; *abundance,* more than enough.

Produce, product, production.—*Produce* is always collective, and is used only of raw products : as, the *produce* of the soil, of the flock. *Product* denotes the result of some operation, usually physical labor. *Production,* meaning "the act of producing," is also applied to a work of literature or art, as a book, a statue, or a painting. "*Product,* in the sense of 'thing produced,' is preferable to *production,* since *production* is also used in an abstract sense." [2]

Prominence, predominance.—*Prominence* means "a standing out from something, so as to be conspicuous." *Predominance* denotes "ascendency," "a superiority in strength or influence," "an over-ruling." There may be many *prominent* traits in a person's character; there can be only one *predominant* trait.

Receipt, recipe.—"*Receipt,* in the sense of 'formula for a pudding, etc.,' is preferable to *recipe,* since *recipe* is commonly restricted to medical prescriptions." [2]

Relative, relation.—"*Relative,* in the sense of 'member of a family,' is preferable to *relation,* since *relation* is also used in an abstract sense." [2]

Requirement, requisite, requisition.—A *requirement* is something required by a person or persons. A *requisite* is something required by the nature of the case. A *requisition* is an authoritative demand or official request for a supply of something.

Resort, recourse, resource.—*Resort* denotes "the act of going to some person or thing"; or "that which is resorted to or habitually visited." *Recourse* means "resort for help or protection." *Resource* denotes "something which is a source of help or support."

Secreting, secretion.—*Secreting* is the act of hiding; *secretion,* a physiological process or fluid.

Sewage, sewerage.—*Sewage* means the contents, *sewerage,* the system, of sewers. .

Situation, site.—"*Situation* embraces all the local aspects and relationships [3] in which a thing is placed. The *site* is confined to the ground on which it is erected or reposes." [4]

---

[1] The Century Dictionary.
[2] A. S. Hill: Principles of Rhetoric, revised edition, p. 19.
[3] Is "relationships" the proper word here?
[4] Smith's Synonyms Discriminated.

Speciality, specialty.—"*Speciality*, in the sense of 'distinctive quality,' is preferable to *specialty*, since *specialty* is also used in the sense of 'distinctive thing.'"[1]

Union, unity.—*Union* is "the joining of two or more things into one." *Unity* means "oneness," "harmony."

Visitant, visitor.—*Visitant* was formerly used to denote a supernatural being; *visitor*, a human one. *Visitant* seems now to be going out of use, *visitor* being used in both senses.

EXERCISE XXII.

Tell the difference in meaning between—

1. He is a person of great ability (capacity).
2. A good character (reputation) is a precious possession.
3. The man seemed to be without conscience (consciousness).
4. The counsel (council) was not wise.
5. It is John's custom (habit) to speak slowly.
6. Her deceit (deception) amazed me.
7. This man is an egoist (egotist).
8. The government does not encourage immigration (emigration).
9. In Mr. E.'s estimate (estimation) the cost of lumber and paint is low.
10. It was only yesterday that I heard of the identification (identity) of the men who robbed Mr. Jones and Mr. Smith.
11. Mr. Gladstone's remark at the banquet was an utterance of great import (importance).
12. This is a remarkable discovery (invention).
13. Carter was nominated by a bare majority (plurality).
14. His death was caused by his own neglect (negligence).
15. The privileges of a novice (novitiate) are not many.
16. What a queer organism (organization)!
17. The expedition has plenty (an abundance) of provisions.
18. He proposes to lay a tax on all English produce (products, productions).
19. He quickly attained prominence (predominance) in the committee.
20. Please copy this receipt (recipe).
21. My relatives (relations) here are charming.

[1] A. S. Hill: Principles of Rhetoric, revised edition, p. 19.

2*

22. Wanted, a boy to do light work in a first-class store. Ability to read and write is a requirement (requisite).

23. The sewage (sewerage) of inland cities presents problems of great difficulty.

24. The site (situation) of the temple is not known.

25. Unity (union) of religious denominations is hoped for by many.

EXERCISE XXIII.

Insert the proper word in each blank, and give the reason for your choice :—

Ability, capacity.

1. The — of the room is not great.

2. They gave, each according to his —.

3. What is — but the power of doing a thing ?

4. Let me drink of Thee according to my —.   (From a prayer.)

5. Some students do not have — to master Greek ; but what most need is — to work persistently.

6. My father does not think Judge X. has much — as a lawyer.

Adherence, adhesion.

7. The — of the parts which were cemented together is still perfect.

8. He showed an obstinate — to false rules of conduct.

9. Marks on the blackboard depend on the — of chalk to the slate.

10. Professor A.'s — to the doctrines of Adam Smith is seen in his last book.

Amount, number, quantity.

11. Our monthly expenditures vary in —.

12. You could see any — of cabs standing in front of the theatre.

13. A great — of books and papers covered the table.

14. Gulliver asked the king of Lilliput for a large — of iron bars and a considerable — of rope.

15. What — of paper is needed for one issue of *Harper's Weekly?*

16. Such a (an) — of sheep as we saw to-day !

17. There is a large — of silver bullion in the Treasury waiting to be coined.

Argument, plea.

18. Every whisper in the court-room was hushed as Mr. N. rose before the jury and began his — in behalf of the prisoner.

19. The — of Smith, when arraigned before the court, was that he had acted in self-defence.

20. The only — available with an east wind is to put on your overcoat.

Balance, remainder, rest.

21. The — of the hour is spent in the study of some poem.

22. I have a — at my banker's.

23. The — of the boys went home.

24. For the — of the week we stayed at home.

25. The account shows a — of $12.46.

26. Give John and Horace four of the six apples; you may have the —.

27. Give the — of our dinner to Tommy, our cat.

Centre, middle.

28. There is a crack running down the — of the wall.

29. A table stood in the — of the room.

30. A path runs through the — of the park.

31. In the — of the garden was a fountain.

32. He parts his hair in the —.

33. The arrow struck the — of the target.

Character, reputation.

34. This man has an excellent — for honesty.

35. Every one admires the — of Washington.

36. Mr. Arnold won great — as a critic.

37. Oh, I have lost my —.

38. The outlaws of Yorkshire were men of loose —.

39. A distinguished general may lose his — through a single blunder.

40. — is an idle and most false imposition; oft got without merit, and lost without deserving.

Complement, compliment.

41. Present my —s to your father.

42. The ship has its — of stores.

43. The — of an angle is the difference between the angle and a right angle.

44. "True friendship loathes such oily —."

45. In the sentence, "He is ill," "ill" is the — of the verb "is."

46.   "This barren verbiage, current among men,
          Light coin, the tinsel clink of —."

Conscience, consciousness.

47. The — of the purity of his motives consoled him for his unpopularity.

48. My — hath a thousand several tongues.

49. I felt a shock, I saw the car topple over, and then I lost —.

Council, counsel.

50. "No man will take —, but every man will take money; therefore money is better than —."—*Swift.*

51. The members of the cabinet form a sort of secret — of the President.

52. Webster was one of the — in the trial of the Knapps for the murder of Captain White.

Custom, habit.

53. De Quincey acquired the — of using opium from first using it to relieve neuralgic pains.

54. Dancing round a May-pole is a — many hundreds of years old.

55. As his — was, he went to the synagogue on the Sabbath.

56. Man is a bundle of —s.

57. Those national —s are best which lead to good —s among the people.

58. A loose life brings a man into —s of dissipation.

59. It was the — of Scotch Highlanders to go bareheaded.

60. It is a good — to rise early, because this will soon become a —.

Deception, deceit.

61. He was guilty of a long course of —.

62. Her character would be charming if it were not for her —.

63. He won my confidence by base —.

64. Deceivers seldom profit by their —.

65. — is of the very nature and essence of sin.

Egotist, egoist.

66. He is an —, for he is always talking about himself.

67. —s are the pest of society; they are always obtruding their ailments on others.

Emigration, immigration.

68. The increase in Chinese — is a matter for serious consideration by the United States Senate.

69. The Chinese government encourages — to America.

70. — is one cause of the rapid growth of our population.

71. The — of the French nobility at the time of the French Revolution was a political blunder.

Enormity, enormousness.

72. The — of the cost of the civil war startles the student of history.

73. Burke drew such a vivid picture of the — of the Nabob of Arcot's crimes that ladies in the audience fainted.

74. Visitors do not at first realize the — of St. Peter's, at Rome.

Esteem, estimate, estimation.

75. In what — is he held by his townsmen ?

76. In my — she is the best of women.

77. We can form an — of the amount of water in the air.

Falseness, falsity.

78. We have already seen the — of that hypothesis.

79. Arnold was despised for his —.

80. Piety is opposed to hypocrisy and —.

81. The prince is in danger of betrayal through the — of his servant.

82. The — of this reasoning is evident.

Identity, identification.

83. The bodies were so disfigured that their — was difficult.

84. In no form of government is there absolute — of interest between the people and their rulers.

Import, importance.

85. He heard the tolling of the bell and trembled at its —.

86. The oath of the President contains three words, all of equal —; namely, that he will "preserve, protect, and defend" the Constitution.

87. He was engaged in business of the highest —.

88. You misunderstood the — of my remarks.

Invention, discovery.

89. Newton's — of the law of gravitation.

90. The — of the telescope was made by Galileo.

91. The — of the properties of the magnetic needle is said to have been made by the Chinese; also, the — of gunpowder.

92. The — of the circulation of blood was made by Harvey.

93. The steam-engine is one of the greatest —s of this age.

94. The — of the telephone is claimed by several persons.

Limit, limitation.

95. All kinds of knowledge have their —s.

96. Titus Quintius was appointed to the command of the army without any —s.

97. Athens insisted upon — of the right to vote.

98. The prisoners were free to roam within certain —s, but their employments were subject to —.

Majority, plurality.

99. If A has 21 votes, B 18, and C 10, A is elected by a —, not a —.

100. Smith had 37 of the 52 votes, a good —.

101. Jones had 20 votes, Smith 14, and Brown 11; Jones therefore was elected by a safe —.

Negligence, neglect.

102.   "Without blame

Or our — we lost her as we came."—*Comus.*

103. Through — to do what ought to be done we soon acquire habits of —.

104. Rescue my poor remains from vile —.

105. The gate has fallen from its hinges, the wooden steps are rotted, and the house shows similar signs of —.

106. — is a grave fault.

Novice, novitiate.

107. For most men a — of silence is profitable before they enter on the business of life.

108. I am young, a — in the trade.

109. It was in this abbey that I served my —.

110. When I was a — in this place, there was here a pious monk.

Organism, organization.

111. Germs of microscopic —s exist abundantly on the surface of all fruits.

112. Lieutenant Peary has completed the — of his arctic expedition.

113. The Jacobin club was a political —.

114. What a complex — the human body is !

Part, portion.

115. A — of my work is done.

116. The younger — of the community.

117. The priests had a — of land assigned them by Pharaoh.

118. The whole is equal to the sum of all its —s.

119. Each received his — of the estate.

120. The lower —s of his body were cold.

121. "This," said he, "is a — of the true cross."

Plenty, abundance.

122. If you do not waste your money, you will have — for your expenses.

123. They did cast in of their — ; but she of her want.

124. The expedition has — of provisions, but none to spare.

125. Last year there was — of corn; it was estimated that we had enough to feed the whole nation for two years.

Produce, product, production.

126. The manufacturers brought their —s to market.

127. The farmers bring their — to town or haul it to the nearest railway station.

128. The apple is especially an American —.

129. Lowell's "Commemoration Ode" is a noble —.

130. Great Britain exports chiefly manufactured —.

131. The component elements of — are labor and capital.

Prominence, predominance.

132. The Indian race is marked by a — of the cheek-bones.

133. The English settlers were *prominent* (*predominant*) in the New World.

134. "Childe Harold" brought Byron into — as a poet.

135. As a man Byron had many *prominent* (*predominant*) faults ; it is not easy to say which one was *prominent* (*predominant*).

Recipe, receipt.

136. Please send me your — for making chocolate ice-cream.

137. Paracelsus furnished a — for making a fairy, but had the delicacy to refrain from using it.

138. He gave me a — for a liniment, which he said was excellent for sprains.

Relative, relation.

139. He has no — in this part of the country.

140. I am the nearest — he has in the world.

Requirement, requisition, requisite.

141. One of the —s in a great commander is coolness.

142. The —s for admission to college vary.

143. One of the —s in a United States minister to France is that he be wealthy, for the salary paid is insufficient to defray the expenses of the minister's social obligations.

144. That locomotive engineers be not color-blind is a just —.

145. The wars of Napoleon were marked by the enormous —s which were made on invaded countries.

Resort, resource, recourse.

146. The woods were her favorite —.

147. The United States has unlimited —s.

148. Newport has long been a — of wealthy society people.

149. When women engage in any art or trade, it is usually as a last —.

150. Hippomenes had — to stratagem.

Secretion, secreting.

151. Jailers are watchful to prevent the — of poison in letters sent to condemned prisoners.

152. Saliva is a —.

Sewage, sewerage.

153. The water of rivers that have received — is not good to drink.

154. The vast and intricate — of Paris is described by Victor Hugo in "Les Miserables."

Situation, site.

155. The — of Samaria is far more beautiful than the — of Jerusalem, though not so grand and wild.

156. Dr. Schliemann made excavations to discover the — of Troy.

157. Our school buildings have a fine —.

158. Has the — of Professor Richard's house been fixed?

159. One of Nebuchadnezzar's temples is thought to have stood on the — of the Tower of Babel.

Specialty, speciality.

160. It is the — of vice that it is selfishly indifferent to the injurious consequences of actions.

161. Diseases of the throat are Dr. Hall's —.

162. Fountain-pens a —.

163. "Toughness" is the — of Salisbury iron; therefore Salisbury iron is much in demand for car-wheels.

Union, unity.

164. How good and how pleasant it is for brethren to dwell together in —.

165. The — of soul and body is ended by death.

166. In the temper of Lord Bacon there was a singular — of audacity and sobriety.

167. This composition lacks —; the writer treats of several distinct subjects.

EXERCISE XXIV.

Tell why the italicized words in the following sentences are misused, and substitute for them better expressions :—

1. The West End Railway Company is the *factor*[1] which can remedy all this.

2. Addison's "Cato" was *a success.*

3. Decoration Day is a fitting *observance* of those who gave their lives for the Union.

4. At the end of each day the *teams*[2] are so broken up that they have to go into the repair-shop, where the carpenter and blacksmith are able to **fix** any part of them.

5. The *majority* of the news is unfavorable.

6. Search-lights would be an indispensable *factor* in a night attack.

7. Bishop Hatto lived in a country where all the *productions* were spoiled by the weather.

8. The *whole* of the stupid boys in Germany struggle to pass this test.

9. The police are looking for the guilty *parties.*

10. A *lot* of men from the country came to town to see the circus.

11. In the shed is a *mixture*[3] of oars, seats, sails, rudders, booms, and gaffs.

12. They had to take the *balance* of his arm off.

13. Addison's essays were a great *factor* in improving the morals of his age.

14. General Manager Payson Tucker at once sent detectives to the scene, and every effort will be made to secure the guilty *parties.*

15. For a few days Coxey's army was *a success* as a show.

16. If it were not for him and a few others of his *ilk* the matter would have been settled long ago.

EXERCISE XXV.[4]

Illustrate by original sentences the correct use of these words :—

Home, party, series, statement, verdict, acceptation, actions, advance, advancement, avocation, completion, allusion, illusion, observation,

---

[1] "Foundations," p. 51.   [2] Ibid., p. 52.   [3] Consult a good dictionary.

[4] To THE TEACHER.—It is easy to underestimate the difficulty which this exercise presents to pupils. In assigning the lesson care must be taken not to call for more of this kind of work than can be done well. Constructing a sentence to illustrate the correct use of a word is a valuable

observance, proposal, proposition, solicitude, solicitation, stimulus, stimulant, capacity, adherence, adhesion, amount, quantity, number, centre, middle, character, complement, compliment, conscience, consciousness, council, counsel, custom, habit, deception, deceit, egoist, emigration, immigration, enormity, enormousness, esteem, estimate, falsity, falseness, import, invention, discovery, limitation, majority, plurality, negligence, neglect, novitiate, organization, organism, produce, product, production, prominence, predominance, recipe, requirement, requisition, requisite, resort, resource, secretion, sewage, sewerage, situation, site, speciality, specialty, union, unity.

exercise, but it is a difficult one; and persons who know the correct use of a word may be put to their wit's end to illustrate that use. It will be well to assign this exercise little by little, while the class works through the definitions and exercises on pages 23–42; or else to select from the list the words on which the class needs most drill. With some pupils it may be wise to omit the exercise entirely.

CHAPTER IV.

OF PRONOUNS

Possessive forms.[1]—No apostrophe is used in forming the possessive case of personal pronouns. We write "ours," "yours," "hers," "its," "theirs." "It's" is a contraction for "it is."

EXERCISE XXVI.

Write from dictation—

1. John's hat is old, yours is new.
2. The bear was lying on its side, dead.
3. The Browns' house is larger than ours, but ours is more convenient than theirs.
4. Yours very respectfully, John Smith.
5. See the yacht! it's coming into the harbor under full sail.
6. Show Mary your doll; it should not grieve you that yours is not so pretty as hers.
7. That fault was not yours.
8. Helen's eyes followed the direction of hers.

Nominative or Objective Case.[2]—There are only seven words in the English language that now have different forms for the nominative and objective cases; therefore it is only in the use of these words that we need to observe any rules about "nominative" or "objective." Since, however, these seven words are more frequently used than any other words, the possibilities of error in choosing between the nominative and the objective are many. Mistakes of this kind are common, and produce a very unpleasant effect on cultivated people. The seven words that have different

---

[1] "Foundations," p. 60.   [2] Ibid., pp. 61–62.

forms for the nominative and objective cases are the following pronouns[1]:—

Nominative.	Objective.	Nominative.	Objective.
I	me	she	her
we	us	they	them
thou	thee	who	whom
he	him		

It is taken for granted that the student has already learned the following principles of syntax:—

1. *Words used absolutely* and the *subjects of finite verbs* should in English be put in the NOMINATIVE form.

2. The *subjects of infinitives* and the *objects* of verbs and prepositions should be in the OBJECTIVE form.

3. Words in *apposition* should be in the same case.

4. The verb "*to be*," or any of its forms (*am, is, are, were,* etc.), does not take an object, but, being equivalent in meaning to the symbol " =," takes the same case after it as before it: the nominative, if the form is "finite"; the objective, if the form is "infinitive" and has a subject of its own. "I know it is *he*," "I know it to be *him*," and "The stranger is thought to be *he*" are grammatically correct.

Sentences like "She invited Mrs. R. and *I* to go driving" are common, even among people generally well-informed. Such mistakes will be avoided if the speaker stops to think what the form would be if the pronoun were not coupled with a noun. No one would think of saying, "She invited *I* to go driving."

Persons who are in doubt as to which form of the pronoun to use often try to avoid the difficulty by using one of the pronouns ending in "-self"—pronouns which have the same form for both the nominative and the objective case. Thus many persons, uncertain whether to use "I" or "me" in the sentence quoted above, would say instead, "She invited Mrs. R. and *myself* to go driving." This is

---

[1] I omit *ye, you,* because they are used interchangeably. I omit also compounds of *who, whom.*

no better than "Mrs. R. and *I*," or "her and *I*." The pronouns in "-self" are properly used only for emphasis or in a reflexive sense.[1] It is right to say: "I will go *myself*"; "Carrie *herself* went to the door"; "God helps those who help *themselves.*" It would be wrong to say, "Harry and *myself* have bought a horse together."

When a pronoun in "-self" is used reflexively, it refers to the subject of the clause in which it stands.

In sentences like "This advice is free to *whoever* will take it," the word ending in "-ever" is the subject of the verb "will take," not the object of the preposition "to." The right form, therefore, is "whoever," not "whomever." The object or, better, the "base" of the preposition "to" is the whole clause, "whoever will take it."

EXERCISE XXVII.

Insert the proper form of pronoun in each blank, and give the reason for your choice:—

I.

I, me, myself.

1. Taking a carriage, my brother and — drove to the east end of Cape Elizabeth.

2. Mr. C. and — walked around the lake by moonlight.

3. The walk gave pleasure to both Mr. C. and —.

4. Between you and —, affairs look dark.

5. The *Star* contains a paper on "Our Streets," which was written by —.

6. He is taller than —.[2]

7. There is, you remember, an old agreement between you and —.

8. May John and — go to the ball-game?

9. Please let John and — go to the ball-game.

10. They met Robert and — in the village.

11. Who is there? Only —.

[1] "Foundations," p. 64.

[2] In sentences like this the correct form will become evident if the speaker mentally completes the sentence thus: He is taller than — *am.* The greater part of the clause after "than" or "as" is generally omitted.

12. To send — away, and for a whole year, too, —, who had never been away from home, was not easy for mother.

13. Will you let Brown and — have your boat?

14. Dr. Holmes shook hands with the girls, — among the rest.

15. Next month my brother and — are going to Bar Harbor.

16. It was — who called to you.

17. I was beside —.

18. Would you go, if you were —?

19. Father bought brother and — tickets for the concert.

20. He said he would bring some flowers to Frances and —.

21. You suffer from headache more than —.

22. We shall soon see which is the better boxer, you or —.

23. Who rang the bell? —.

24. The taller man was supposed to be —.

25. Every one has gone except you and —.

26. The world will rest content with such poor things as you and —.

27. He was a sublimer poet than —.

28. Was it — that you saw?

29. How can you thus address me, —, who am your friend?

30. Let you and — go for berries alone, if he will not go with us.

31. There is no one here but you and —.

32. Is it — you wish to see?

33. He said that you and — might go.

34. Oh, no; it couldn't have been —.

35. Harry left word for you and — to come to his room.

36. Other girls have books as well as —.

37. Its being — should make no difference.

38. Young Macdonald and — went to New York last Thursday.

39. She knew it to be — by my gait.

II.

We, us, ourselves.

1. Our friends and — are going out to-night.

2. He has come to take our friends and — driving.

3. They are wiser than —, since they are older.

4. They will lose more than — by the failure of the bank.

5. The Germans are better plodders than —.

6. It may have been — who (whom) you saw.

7. — boys are having a fine time.

8. Have you seen the picture of — three girls in a boat, taken by Mr. B. ?

9. There are five hundred miles between father and —.

10. They know that as well as —.

11. They don't succeed any better than —.

12. They as well as — were disappointed.

13. — ought not to get angry when others criticise — for faults which — — freely acknowledge.

14.
"It is not fit for such as —
To sit with rulers of the land."

III.
Thou, thee, thyself.

1. I will not learn my duty from such as —.

2. If they rob only such as —, I hold them right honest folk.

3. Love — last.

4.
"The nations not so blest as —
Must in their turn to tyrants fall."

5. " Wife, dost — know that all the world seems queer except — and me; and sometimes I think even — art a little queer ?"

6.
"Hail to —, blithe spirit;
Bird — never wert."

IV.
He, him, himself.

1. There is a difference between an employer and — who (whom) he employs.

2. John — wrote that letter.

3. You are nearly as tall as —.

4. All wore dress suits except Charles and —.

5. I know that it was —.

6. I knew it to be —.

7. — being young, they tried to deceive him.

8. It was either — or his brother that called.

9. What were you and — talking about ?

10. I can run as fast as —.

11. — who had always protected her, she now saw dead at her feet.

12. — and his father are in business together.

13. She is as good as —.

14. I should never have imagined it to be —.

15. Boys like you and — are expected to do what is right without being told.

16. Yes, I told them what you said, — among the rest.
17. I did as well as —.
18. It was Joseph, — whom Pharaoh made prime-minister.
19. Let — who made thee answer that.
20. Whom can I trust, if not — ?

V.
She, her, herself.

1. Before leaving Mary we saw — and her baggage safe on the train.
2. — and her two cousins have been visiting us.
3. I would not go to town alone, if I were —.
4. It was not — but her sister that you met yesterday.
5. You are as old as —.
6. — and I are not in the same class.
7. Was it — that did it?
8. I cannot let you and — sit together.
9. You play the violin better than —.
10. Such girls as — are not good companions.
11. I am certain that it was —.
12. Girls like — are not good company.
13. If any one is embarrassed, it will not be —.
14. If any one is late it will be sure to be —.

VI.
They, them, themselves.

1. — and their children have left town.
2. We shall soon be as poor as —.
3. Yes, it was —.
4. I do not know whether the Macdonalds are Scotch or Irish; but I thought the Scotch family alluded to might be —.
5. The mischievous boys you speak of could not have been —, for — were at home.

VII.
Who, whom, whoever, whomever.

1. — are you going to give that to?
2. — do men say that I am?
3. — do men think me to be?
4. — am I supposed to be?
5. — do you think will be elected?
6. — do you think they will select?

7. I do not know — to compare him to.

8. Tell me in sadness — is she you love ?

9. — are you going to call on next ?

10. How can we tell — to trust ?

11. — is that for ?

12. Elect — you like.

13. — did you see at the village ?

14. — did you say went with you ?

15. Do you know — you can get to take my trunk ?

16. — were you talking to just now ?

17. I do not know — you mean.

18. Do you remember — he married ?

19. We will refer the question to — you may select as arbitrator.

20. — can this letter be from ?

21. He is a man — I know is honest.[1]

22. He is a man — I know to be honest.[1]

23. — do you take me to be ?

24. — did you expect to see ?

25. Can't you remember — you gave it to ?

26. I saw a man — I have no hesitation in saying was Julian H.

27. We like to be with those — we love and — we know love us, let them be — they may.

28. — do you think it was that called ?

29. He confided his plan to those — he thought were his friends.

30. He confided his plan to those — he thought he could trust.

31. We recommend only those — we think can pass the examinations, and — we know will do their best.

32. — do you think she looks like ?

33. One letter was from an applicant — I afterwards learned had been out of a position for two years.

34. — did you suppose it was ?

35. Opposite him was a handsome man — John knew must be Kathleen's uncle.

36. A witness — the counsel for the defence expected would be present was kept away by illness.

---

[1] In the first of these sentences the pronoun to be supplied is the subject of "is honest," and "I know" is parenthetical. In the second sentence, the pronoun to be supplied is the subject of "to be honest," which is the complement of "I know."

3

37. A witness — the counsel expected to be present was kept away.

38. Give it to — seems to need it most.

39. — does he think it could have been ?

40. They have found the child — they thought was stolen.

41. Mr. Morton, —, it is announced, the President has appointed minister to France, has a house at Saratoga.

42. Miss C. married an old gentleman — they say is very wealthy.

43. The king offered to give his daughter in marriage to — would kill the terrible monster.

44. — do you think I saw in Paris ?

45. — are you going to vote for ?

46. They left me ignorant as to — it was.

47. We were betrayed by those — we thought would die for us.

48. I don't know — to ask for.

49. I know — it is I serve.

50. The President has appointed Mr. L., — he thinks will show himself well fitted for the position.

51. One member of the committee was absent —, it was asserted by the minority, would have voted in the negative.

52. The officer addressed the woman, — he plainly saw to be very much out of place there.

53. — did he refer to, he (him) or I (me)?

54. Ariel was a spirit — a certain witch had shut up in a tree.

55. Seated on an upright tombstone, close to him, was a strange, unearthly figure, — Gabriel felt at once was no being of this world.

56. He then got into the carriage to sit with the man — he had been told was Morgan.

57. If she did not take after Anne, — did she take after ?

Pronouns before **Verbal Nouns.**[1]—Grammarians distinguish three kinds of words formed from verbs by the adding of "-ing."

"She goes about her work *singing* gayly." In this sentence "singing" partakes of the nature of an adjective (describing "she") and is called a PARTICIPLE.

"*Singing* blithely is better than *moaning* sadly." "By

[1] "Foundations," pp. 62–64.

cheerily *singing* pretty songs she keeps our spirits up." In these sentences the words in "-ing" are nouns, but like verbs they are modified by adverbs, and one of them has an object. Such words in "-ing" are called GERUNDS.

"The blithe *singing* of Katharine helps to make home happy." Here, too, "singing" is a noun; but now it is modified by an adjective, and is preceded by "the" and followed by "of." Such words, derived from the old verbal noun in "-ung," are called VERBAL NOUNS.

A noun or pronoun used before a gerund to denote the subject of the action named by it, is put in the possessive case. The reason for this becomes evident if, in the sentence "Do you remember *him* (*his*) *preaching* here two years ago?" we substitute for the noun "preaching" another noun, "sermon"; thus, "Do you remember *him* (*his*) *sermon* here two years ago?" If "preaching" were a participle, "him" would be right; as in the sentence, "He speaks so loud that I can hear *him preaching* a square away."

When a verbal noun is preceded by "the" it should be followed by "of"; conversely, when it is followed by "of" it should be preceded by "the," unless it is made definite by some other modifier; as, "*Her singing of* this song was applauded heartily."

EXERCISE XXVIII.

Which of the following forms is preferable?   Give the reason:—

1. I heard of him (his) coming home.
2. What do you think of Marguerite (Marguerite's) studying Latin?
3. Have you any doubt of Kathleen (Kathleen's) being happy?
4. We saw the lady (lady's) crossing the street.
5. Do you remember my (me) speaking to you about your penmanship?
6. We saw the old miser (miser's) sitting alone in front of his hut.
7. What is the good of your (you) going now?
8. There was no doubt of him (his) being promoted.

9. Trust to me (my) being on time.

10. Are you surprised at it (its) being him (he)?

11. No doubt his example will be followed by others, with the consequence of the country (country's) being overrun by tramps.

12. Look at him (his) reading a book.

13. The delay was caused by us (our) missing the train.

14. I found him (his) reading Idyls of the King.

15. This may lead to Harry (Harry's) getting a position.

16. We did not see the house (house's) burning.

17. You (your) writing the letter so neatly secured for you the position.

18. The man's (man) breaking jail is evidence of his guilt.

19. What do you think about this cloth (cloth's) wearing well?

20. We must insist upon every man (man's) doing his duty.

21. Mr. R.'s (Mr. R.) having come to town will soon be known.

22. There is prospect of the Senate (Senate's) passing the tariff bill.

23. What use is there in a man (man's) swearing?

24. His parents are opposed to him (his) playing football.

25. No one ever saw fat men (men's) heading a riot.

26. A fierce struggle ensued, ending in the intruder (intruder's) being worsted.

27. Professor C. relies on us (our) passing our examinations.

28. I felt my heart (heart's) beating faster.

29. There is no use in me (my) trying to learn Hebrew.

30. I enjoy nothing more than the sight of a yacht (yacht's) sailing in a stiff breeze.

31. Brown (Brown's) being a manufacturer prevented his election.

EXERCISE XXIX.

Distinguish in meaning between the following sentences:—

1. The man (man's) asking to be allowed to vote started a quarrel.

2. Did you see him (his) riding?

3. I had to laugh at John (John's) riding a bicycle.

4. Think of me (my) eating frogs' legs.

5. Much depends on the teacher (teacher's) correcting the papers.

6. Did you watch him (his) entering the room?

7. Did you hear Ruth (Ruth's) singing?

8. No one ever heard of that man (man's) running for office.

EXERCISE XXX.

Explain the faults in the following sentences and correct them in several ways :—

1. He read the parable about the sowing the seed.
2. Good writing depends on reading of good books.
3. Youth is the time for the forming the character.
4.   "In building of chaises, I tell you what,
    There is always somewhere a weakest spot."
5. He would not aid me so much as by the lifting a hand.
6. Groaning of prisoners and clanking of chains were heard.
7. By the obtaining wisdom you will command esteem.
8. By reading of good books his style was improved.
9. The taking things by force is apt to make trouble.
10. A more careful guarding the prisoners would have prevented this accident.

Choice of Relative Pronouns.'— *Who* is now used only of persons; *which*, of things; *that*, of either persons or things. As a rule, euphony decides between *who* or *which* and *that*.

"*Who* is used chiefly of persons (though also often of the higher animals), *which* almost only of animals and things (in old English also of persons), and *that* indifferently of either, except after a preposition, where only *who* [*whom*] or *which* can stand. Some recent authorities teach that only *that* should be used when the relative clause is limiting or defining: as, the man *that* runs fastest wins the race; but *who* or *which* when it is descriptive or co-ordinating: as, this man, *who* ran fastest, won the race; but, though present usage is perhaps tending in the direction of such a distinction, it neither has been nor is a rule of English speech, nor is it likely to become one, especially on account of the impossibility of setting *that* after a preposition; for to turn all relative clauses into the form 'the house *that* Jack lived *in*' (instead of 'the house *in which* Jack lived') would be intolerable. In good punctuation the defining relative is distinguished (as in the examples above) by never taking a comma before it, whether it be *who* or *which* or *that*. Wherever *that* could be properly used, but only there, the relative may be, and very often is,

---

[1] "Foundations," pp. 60, 65, 67–69.

omitted altogether; thus, the house Jack built or lived in; the man he built it for."[1]

When the antecedent includes both persons and things, *that* is preferable to *who* or *which.*

"When the antecedent is a neuter noun not personified, a writer should prefer *of which* to *whose,* unless euphony requires the latter."[2]

What, as a relative pronoun, is equivalent to "that which." It is never used with an antecedent, since the antecedent is included in the meaning of the word.

The word *as* is a relative pronoun only after "such" or "same." After "such" the proper relative is "as"; after "same" it is "as" or "that." "*Same as* usually expresses identity of kind, *same that* absolute identity, except in contracted sentences where *same as* is alone found: cf. 'he uses the same books *as* you do,' 'he uses the same books *that* you do,' 'he uses the same books *as* you.'"[3]

EXERCISE XXXI.

Insert the proper relative pronoun in the blanks in the following sentences, giving the reason for your choice:—

1. Man is the only animal — can talk.

2. There are many persons —, though they be starving, will not beg.

3. This is the malt — lay in the house — Jack built.

4. I will have no such son-in-law — thinks himself better than I (me).[4]

5. Tennyson, — was the foremost poet of England, died in 1892.

6. Time — is lost is never found again.

7. There are many — saw him fall.

8. The soldiers and cannon — you saw belong to the French army.

9. Who — hears Professor C. read the court scene from "Pickwick" does not go away delighted ?

[1] The Century Dictionary.   [2] "Foundations," p. 68.
[3] Murray's Dictionary.   [4] See note, p. 48.

10. She is the same girl since her marriage — she was before it.

11. The dog dropped the bone, — then fell into the water.

12. He — does all — he can does all — can be expected.

13. Her hair, — was dark brown, was gathered in a Grecian knot.

14. Tears, such — angels weep, burst forth.

15. I have a water-spaniel, — follows me everywhere.

16. The horse — ran away with Harry belonged to Mr. H.

17. Such — I have I give you.

18. This is the same man — I spoke of.

19. The diamond, — is so highly prized, is pure carbon, — in the form of charcoal is familiar to all.

20. All the men and horses — were on the transports were drowned when the vessels sank.

21. The murdered innocents at Bethlehem were martyrs — died for a king — they had never seen.

22. What pleased me most, and — has been most frequently mentioned by visitors to the fair, was the beauty of the buildings.

23. I trusted to my dog, — knew the way better than I did.

24. Dr. A.'s report shows the same record of efficiency — has always characterized his conduct.

25. Shakespeare was the greatest poet — the English race has produced.

26. He spends all — he earns.

27. The review of the National Guard of Pennsylvania by Sheridan was the largest military display — I have seen.

28. Was it you or the wind — made those noises?

29. We have invited the same girls — were here yesterday.

30. It was the cat, not I or the wind, — frightened you.

31. The dog — my brother gave me ran away.

32. Do you know that man — is just entering the car?

33. Such eloquence — was heard in the Senate in those days!

34. He held the same political opinions — his illustrious friend.

35.   "Nature ever faithful is
              To such — trust her faithfulness."

36. Is this a dagger — I see before me?

37. We saw the men and arms — were captured.

Either or Any one, Neither or No one.[1]—*Either* means

---

[1] "Foundations," pp. 69–70.

"one of the two"; *neither,* "no one of the two." When more than two persons or things are spoken of, "any one" is preferable to "either," and "no one" to "neither."

EXERCISE XXXII.

Insert the proper word or words ("either," "neither," "any one," "no one") in each blank in the following sentences:—

1. Only three persons saw the fight, and — of them would testify.
2. Has — of you two gentlemen a fountain-pen?
3. I defy any candid and clear thinker to deny in the name of inductive science — of these six propositions.
4. When two persons disagree, it is not likely that — is altogether wrong.
5. Has — of you who have just come from the ball-field seen Julian?
6. I have several histories of France, — of which will give you the information.
7. Here come Harry and Arthur; — will go to get it for you.
8. Give it to the six successful students or to — of them.

Each or all.[1]—*Each* denotes every one of any number taken one by one; *all* denotes the entire number taken together.

EXERCISE XXXIII.

Insert the proper word ("each," "all") in each blank:—

1. — gave me his (their) hand(s).
2. — of the workmen received two dollars a day.
3. — of the children has (have) his (their) peculiar traits.
4. — of the members is (are) entitled to a vote.
5. He gave an apple to — of us.
6. Did your father bring the boat to Harry? No, he brought it to — of us.
7. — of them did his (their) duty.

Change of Pronoun.[2]—In referring to the same person or thing a writer should not change from one pronoun to another.

The possessive of "one" is "one's" (not "his"), except

<hr>

[1] "Foundations," p. 70.   [2] Ibid., pp. 72–74.

in such expressions as "every one," "no one," "many a one." The reflexive is "one's self."

It is a common but serious fault to begin to write in the third person, and then to change to the first or second.

EXERCISE XXXIV.

Fill the blanks with the proper pronouns:—

1. The Second Regiment of the National Guard, — was sent to Pittsburg during the strike, and — is now in camp at Gettysburg, has six hundred members.

2. John started to school last Monday; we wish — success.

3. Proud damsel, — shalt be proudly met. I withdraw my pretensions to — hand until I return from the war.

4. As — hast said, — lands are not endangered. But hear me before I leave —.

5. The cat was crouching on the piazza and we were watching —. Suddenly — tail twitched nervously and — prepared to spring.

6.   "Ere you remark another's sin,
           Bid — conscience look within."

7. At first one is likely to wonder where the boats are, since on entering the grove — is (are) able to see only a small cabin.

8. Dost — talk of revenge? — conscience, it seems, has grown dull.

9. As a Christian — art obliged to forgive — enemy.

10. Did you never bear false witness against — neighbor?

11. The shepherd ran after a sheep and caught — just as — was jumping over a hedge.

12. The hen gathered — brood under — wing.

13. This is a book which I have never read, but one — is recommended by Mrs. M.

EXERCISE XXXV.

1. Write the following note in clear and correct form, using the third person :—

"Mr. Smith presents his compliments to Mr. Jones, and finds he has a cap which isn't mine. So, if you have a cap which isn't his, no doubt they are the ones."[1]

[1] Quoted in "Foundations," p. 74.

3*

2. Write a formal note in the third person, asking an acquaintance to dine with you at a certain hour in order that you may consult with him about some matter of importance.

3. Write a note in the third person accepting or declining this invitation.

4. Write a formal note in the third person to some gentleman to whom you have a letter of introduction, asking when it will be convenient to have you call.

5. Write a notice in the third person offering a reward for the recovery of a lost article.

Singular or Plural Pronouns.[1]—The rule that a pronoun should be in the same number as its antecedent is violated most commonly in connection with such expressions as "any one," "each," "either," "every," "man after man," "neither," "nobody." Grammatically such expressions are singular.

"He" ("his," "him") may stand for mankind in general and include women as well as men.

EXERCISE XXXVI.

Fill the blanks with the proper pronouns:—

1. Many a brave man met — death in the war.
2. Has everybody finished — exercise?
3. If any one has not finished let — hold up — hand.
4. It is true that this is a free country; but that does not mean that every one may do as — please (pleases).
5. Either John or Harry will let you look on — book.
6. Let each take — turn.
7. If anybody but John had come, we would not have admitted —.
8. Any one who wishes may have a ribbon to wear in — buttonhole.
9. Neither Bois-Guilbert nor Front de Bœuf found himself (themselves) a match for the unknown knight who challenged —.
10. Every kind of animal has — own proper food.
11. Not an officer, not a private escaped getting — clothes wet.

---

[1] "Foundations," pp. 75–76.

12. The Senate has (have) instructed — conferees to yield to the demand of the conferees of the House of Representatives.

13. Everybody has possessions of some kind which — prize (prizes) highly.

14. It is a shame that each of the men, when — draw (draws) — pay, take (takes) it to the tavern.

15. Will either of you gentlemen lend me — (third person) pencil?

16. Two men saw the deed; but neither would tell what — saw.

17. Every one should be careful of the feelings of those around —.

18. Each of the pupils has (have) — own dictionary.

19. Nobody went out of — way to make her feel at home.

20. Neither Charles nor his brother ate — breakfast this morning.

21. Everybody goes to bed when — please (pleases).

22. The committee has handed in — report.

23. The senior class has elected — class-day speakers.

24. If any one wishes to see me let — call at my office.

25. Either Florence or Grace will lend you — fan.

26. Every one must judge of — own feelings.

27. Whoever loves — school should do — best to elevate the school tone.

28. A person who is rude in — table manners will be disliked.

29. Nobody in — senses ever thinks of doing that.

30. Each one as before will chase — favorite phantom.

31. She laughs like one out of — mind.

32. Everybody was on deck amusing —self (selves) as best — could.

33. No one should marry unless — has (have) the means of supporting —self (selves) and — family.

34. Probably everybody is eloquent at least once in — life.

35. Everybody rises early and goes on deck, where — inhale (inhales) the fresh salt air.

36. Each of the gentlemen offered — assistance.

37. Nobody but a fool would have left — money in such a place.

38. Anybody wishing to sell — bicycle will please call at No. 267.

39. Franklin and Collins started off together, each with very little money in — pockets.

40. In the time of Franklin's great-great-grandfather, if a person was caught using an English Bible — was (were) treated as a heretic.

41. Nobody should praise —self (selves).

42. Neither the merchant nor the lawyer made —self (selves) rich.

43. Every man and every boy received — wages.

44. When the carnival comes off. everybody who owns a boat, or who can borrow one, decorates it as best — can with lanterns and trimmings.

45. Every cowboy carries a pistol and knows how to use it very quickly; — also has (have) a knife stuck in — belt, in the use of which — is (are) very expert.

46. Everybody's heart is open, you know, when — has (have) recently escaped from severe pain.

Omitted Pronouns.[1]— The omission of necessary pronouns—an omission especially common in business letters —cannot be justified on the ground of brevity.

EXERCISE XXXVII.

Insert the omitted pronouns in—

1. After twenty-two years' experience announce the opening of my new store. Hope to serve the public better by presenting new ideas. Would invite inspection.

2. Have received manuscript, but not had time to examine. Will take up in a few days. If good, will publish.

3. Dr. Jones and wife occupy the front room.

4. My inability to get employment, and destitute condition, depressed me.

5. She didn't trouble to make any excuse to her husband.

6. Accept thanks for lovely present. Hope we may have the pleasure of using together in the near future.

Redundant Pronouns.—A vulgarism not often seen in writing, but common in conversation, consists in the use of an unnecessary pronoun after the subject of a sentence. Thus,

Teacher: Who was Benjamin Franklin ?

Pupil: Benjamin Franklin, *he* was a great American philosopher and statesman.

[1] "Foundations," pp. 77, 78.

CHAPTER V.

OF VERBS

Correct and Incorrect Forms.[1] — It is not enough to learn by heart the "principal parts" of a verb; the habit of using them correctly should be acquired. The following verb-forms are often misused :—

Present.	*Past Indicative.*	*Past Participle.*
awake (intransitive)	awoke	awaked
begin	began	begun
beseech	besought	besought
blow	blew	blown
bid ("to order," "to greet")	băde	bidden or bid
bid (at auction)	bid	bidden or bid
break	broke	broken[2]
burst	burst	burst
choose	chose	chosen
come	came	come
dive	dived	dived
do	did	done
drive	drove	driven
eat	ate	eaten
flee	fled	fled
fly	flew	flown
freeze	froze	frozen
forget	forgot	forgotten
get	got	got[3]
go	went	gone
hang	hung, hanged[4]	hung, hanged[4]
lay ("to cause to lie")	laid	laid

[1] "Foundations," pp. 78–81, 91–93.
[2] "Broke," as a form of the past participle, is still found in verse.
[3] "Gotten" is an old form not sanctioned by the best modern usage.
[4] "Clothes are 'hung' on the line; men are 'hanged' on the gallows."— "Foundations," p. 79.

Present.	Past Indicative.	Past Participle.
lie ("to recline")	lay	lain
plead	pleaded	pleaded
prove	proved	proved[1]
ride	rode	ridden
rise (intransitive)	rose	risen
raise (transitive)	raised	raised
run	ran	run
see	saw	seen
set ("to put"; of the sun, moon, etc., "to sink")	set	set
sit	sat	sat
shake	shook	shaken
shoe	shod	shod
show	showed	shown
speak	spoke	spoken
slay	slew	slain
steal	stole	stolen
take	took	taken
throw	threw	thrown
wake (transitive)	woke	waked
write	wrote	written

In using the verbs *drink, ring, shrink, sing, sink, spring, swim,* it seems better to confine the forms in " a " to the preterite tense, and the forms in " u " to the past participle: as, "The bell *rang* five minutes ago"; "Yes, the bell has *rung*."[2]

The following forms also should be distinguished :—

Present.	Past.	Participle.
alight ("to get down from," "to dismount")	alighted	alighted
light ("to ignite," "to shed light on")	lighted[2]	lighted[3]
light ("to settle down as a bird from flight," or "to come upon by chance")	lighted or lit	lighted or lit

[1] "'Proven' is borrowed from the Scotch legal dialect."—"Foundations," p. 92.　　　　　　　　　　　　　　　　　　[2] Ibid., p. 91.

[3] "'Lighted' seems preferable to 'lit'; but 'lit' is used by some writers of reputation."—Ibid., p. 92.

EXERCISE XXXVIII.

Change the italicized verbs in these sentences to the past tense:—

1. The guests *begin* to go home.
2. I *beseech* you to hear me.
3. The wind *blows* furiously.
4. The steward *bids* me say that supper is ready.
5. Mr. O. *bids* forty-two dollars for the picture.
6. George *dives* better than any other boy in the crowd.
7. I *do* it myself.
8. They *eat* their supper as if they were half starved.
9. The enemy *flee* before us.
10. The door *flies* open.
11. The wild goose *flies* southward in the autumn.
12. He *flees* at the smell of powder.
13. The Susquehanna river *overflows* its banks.
14. The workmen *lay* the rails for the track with great care.
15. Obedient to the doctor's directions, she *lies* down an hour every day.
16. Our cat *lies* on the rug by the hour watching for mice.
17. The cows *lie* under the trees in the meadow.
18. Helen *comes* in and *lays* her coat on a chair.
19. The envoys *plead* with Cæsar earnestly.
20. Both short-stop and pitcher *run* for the ball.
21. He *runs* up to Mr. C. as if to strike him.
22. I *see* two cannon and a company of infantry.
23. Harry *sees* me coming.
24. The negro women *set* their baskets on their heads.
25. They *sit* in the third pew from the front.
26. Mr. N. always *shoes* my pony.
27. The savages who *live* on this island *slay* their captives.
28. The catcher often *throws* the ball to the second base.
29. The sun *wakes* me early.
30. The bell *rings* at seven o'clock.
31. The stag *drinks* his fill.
32. She *sings* sweetly.
33. Armed men *spring* up on all sides.
34. Tom *swims* very well indeed.
35. The vessel *sinks* with all on board.
36. The colonel and his staff *alight* in front of the general's tent.

37. He *lights* the lamp with a splint.
38. On the trees a crested peacock *lights*.

EXERCISE XXXIX.

Change these sentences so that the italicized verbs will be either in the perfect tense or in the passive voice:—

1. The sleeper *awakes*.
2. The Gauls *beseech* Cæsar to be merciful.
3. The wind *blows* my papers off the table.
4. Ethel *broke* her arm.
5. His wrongdoing *breaks* my heart.
6. The pressure of the water *breaks* the pipes.
7. They *choose* Mr. W. to be their chairman.
8. The enemy *come* in force.
9. The boys *dive* three times.
10. John *is driving* the cows out of the corn.
11. The boys *are eating* their supper.
12. An absconding cashier *flees* to Canada.
13. A robin *flies* to the vines by my window.
14. The Ohio river *overflows* its banks.
15. The water in my pitcher *froze*.
16. I *forget* his name.
17. He *gets* along fairly well.
18. They *go* by steamer.
19. The sheriff *hangs* the condemned man.
20. The maid *hangs* up my cloak.
21. I *lie* on the couch twenty minutes to rest.
22. Tramps *lie* by the road below the gate.
23. Boys *lay* traps for hares.
24. They *lay* burdens on me greater than I can bear.
25. They *plead* their cause well.
26. This *proves* the truth of my assertion.
27. He *rides* alone from Litchfield to Waterbury.
28. A mist *rises* before my eye.
29. I *see* the President often.
30. I *set* the lamp on the table.
31. He *sits* by the hour talking politics.
32. Rab *shakes* the little dog by the neck.
33. He *is shoeing* my horse.

34. This fact clearly *shows* the prisoner's guilt.

35. He *speaks* his declamation well.

36. They *slay* their prisoners.

37. He *stole* my watch.

38. Some one *takes* my hat.

39. He *throws* cold water on my plan.

40. He *writes* home.

41. He *wakes* me every night by his restlessness.

NOTE.—If the teacher thinks that the class needs more drill of this kind, Exercises XXXVIII. and XXXIX. may be reversed, that is, the verbs in XXXVIII. may be changed to perfect or passive forms; the verbs in XXXIX. to the past tense. If this is done, some of the sentences will have to be slightly recast. In the next exercise drill on the same forms is continued in a different way.

EXERCISE XL.

Insert the proper form in each of the blanks in the following sentences:—

Awake, wake.

1. I — at six o'clock this morning; I have — at about the same time ever since I have been at school.

2. Lord Byron one morning — to find himself famous. A certain Mr. Peck — one day last week to find that the *Nation* had made him notorious.

3. A few nights ago Mr. Michael Dixon was — by a burglar in his bedroom.

4. He — me an hour before time.

5. Have you — your brother?

6. He — as I opened the door.

Begin.

7. He had — his speech before we arrived.

8. The Senators — to ask him questions. Then he — to be confused.

Bid.

9. When the Major passed us he — us good-morning very politely.

10. Father has for— us to go there.

Blow.

11. Before the sunset gun was fired the bugler — a strain on his bugle.

12. The top-mast of the sloop was — away.

Break.

13. Did you hear that Waldo has — his leg?
14. The window was — by Jack.

Burst.

15. When the South Sea bubble —, thousands of families were made poor.
16. The cannon was — by an overcharge of powder.

Choose.

17. If they had — him, they would have — more wisely.
18. A better day for a drive could not have been —.

Come.

19. Harry — running up to me and asked me to lend him my cap.

Dive.

20. The loon saw the flash of my gun and —.
21. It had — several times before.

Do.

22. I know he — it; for it could not have been — by any one else.
23. Ask him why he — it.

Drive.

24. He was — out of town by his indignant neighbors.
25. This stake has been — in deep.

Eat.

26. The scraps were — up by the dog.
27. The men have — their dinner.

Flee, fly, flow.

28. During the night the river had over— its banks.
29. Benedict Arnold was forced to — the country. He — to England.
30. The birds have — away.
31. The guilty man has —. He — with his family to Mexico.
32. Our meadow was over— during the freshet.
33. The yacht — like a bird before the wind.
34. The lotus-eaters watched the gleaming river as it — seaward.
35. It had — through the same channel hundreds of years.
36. The terrified savages — to the mountains.
37. They shall — from the wrath to come.
38. The plantations along the Mississippi are over—.

Forget.

39. Once Sydney Smith, being asked his name by a servant, found to his dismay that he had — his own name.

40. Maude is late; she must have — the time.

Freeze.

41. I thought my ears were —.

42. He would have — to death if he had not been found by the St. Bernard dogs.

Get.

43. They have — home.

44. Whenever any milk was wanted it could be — from the magic pitcher.

45. Grace has — three seats for to-night.

46. Franklin asked the boy where he had — the bread.

Go.

47. The price of coal has — up since last year.

48. He would have — with us if he had been invited.

Hang.

49. Judas, overwhelmed with remorse, went and — himself.

50. In olden times in England a man was — for stealing a sheep.

Lay, lie.

51. Two men — under the hay-stack all yesterday morning. They must have — there all night.

52. — down and rest.

53. He came in and — his books on his desk.

54. After he — down he remembered that he had left his pocket-book —ing by the open window.

55. He played until he was so tired that he had to — down.

56. He has — himself at full length on the grass.

57. You had better — down for a while after dinner.

58. I have — down, and I feel rested.

59. I — down an hour ago to take a nap.

60. The scene of "The Lady of the Lake" is — in the lake region of Scotland.

61. The tired lambs — down to rest.

62. Darkness settled down while the soldiers — behind the breast-works.

63. Had you not better — down a while?

64. After they had been —ing silent for an hour, the command

was given to prepare for a march; afterward the men — down again and waited for the next order.

65. When Romeo saw Juliet —ing in the casket, he — down by her side and drank the poison. When Juliet awoke, seeing Romeo —ing beside her dead, she took a sword which — near and killed herself.

Plead.

66. He — tearfully to be set free, but his captors were firm.
67. Yesterday he — "not guilty."

Prove.

68. It cannot be — that Mars is inhabited.
69. He thinks that the prisoner's innocence has been —.

Ride.

70. We had — only a short distance when rain began to fall.
71. Have you ever — on a bicycle?

Rise, raise.

72. She could not get her bread to —.
73. The price of corn has —.
74. I — so that I might look around.
75. The students — him upon their shoulders.

Run.

76. You look as if you had — all the way home.
77. He — up to me and asked what time it was.
78. He said some thief had taken his coat and had — away with it.

See.

79. Charlie, who has just come in, says he — two suspicious looking men near the barn.
80. Yes, I — him an hour ago.
81. That is the best dog I ever —.

Set, sit.

82. Please — still while I try to find her.
83. The old man was —ting in his easy-chair.
84. He — out for Boston day before yesterday.
85. — down and talk awhile.
86. The sun —s at six o'clock twice a year.
87. I — the basket on a rock while I went to the spring.
88. We — with our friends at the table for over an hour.
89. In which seat did you — ?

90. I am —ting in my study by the window.

91. The children are dreadfully sunburnt; yesterday they — in the sun on the beach all the morning.

92. Just — down, till I call her.

93. Annie, I have — the pitcher on the table.

94. He has — there all the evening.

95. We were all —ting round the fire. .

96. I had to — up all night.

97. The farmer after felling the tree found that it had fell (fallen) on a —ting hen that had laid (lain) her eggs under its branches.

Shake.

98. All the restraints of home had been — off long before.

99. John — the tree; Lida picked up the nuts.

100. After they had — off the dust, they entered the house.

Shoe.

101. Go, ask Mr. N. whether he has — the horses yet.

102. He says he — them an hour ago.

Show.

103. They have — their good intention.

104. Has Edward — you his yacht? Yes, he — it to me this morning.

Speak.

105. English is — in many parts of the world.

106. After he had — a half-hour we had to leave.

Slay.

107. David — Goliath with a pebble.

108. A brave man never boasts of having — his thousands.

Steal.

109. He thinks the horse was —.

110. Some one has — my purse.

Take.

111. I found upon inquiry that I had mis— the house.

112. Yesterday she — me home with her.

113. You look as if you had — root there.

Throw.

114. He — the ball to me and I — it back.

115. The Governor's son was — from his pony this morning.

Write.

116. I think he should have — and told us.

117. He — for the book two days ago.

118. She has — for samples.

Drink.

119. The toast was — with great enthusiasm.

120. Then they — to the health of the President.

121. He had once — sour wine and slept in the secret chamber at Wolf's Crag.

Ring.

122. The fire bell — twice last night. It had not — for two months before.

123. Has the last bell — ?

Sing.

124. The choir boys — the "Hallelujah Chorus" from "The Messiah." It seemed to me that they had never — so well.

Sink.

125. The steamer struck an iceberg and — with all on board.

126. They have — two wells, but have got (gotten) no water.

Spring.

127. The grass — up like magic last night.

128. Homer describes a race of men who — from the gods.

Swim.

129. I once — three-quarters of a mile without stopping.

130. Having — the river, the fugitives plunged into the forest.

EXERCISE XLI.

Illustrate by original sentences the proper use of the past indicative and the past participle of each of the following verbs, thus: A swallow FLEW *into my room, but before I recovered from my surprise it had* FLOWN *out again. Give to the sentences variety :—*

Awake, beat, begin, beseech, blow, bid (to order), bid (to offer), break, burst, choose, come, dive, do, drive, eat, flee, fly, flow, forget, freeze, get, go, hang, lay, lie (to recline), plead, prove, ride, rise, run, see, set, sit, shake, shoe, show, speak, slay, steal, take, throw, wake, write.

Contractions.[1]—Some writers hold that in careful writing contracted forms should be avoided; but all are agreed that in conversation some contractions, if correctly used, are natural and proper. The conversation of a person who never said "can't" for "can not," "don't" for "do not," or "doesn't" for "does not," would seem stiff. Care should, however, be taken not to use plural contractions for singular, or singular for plural. *Don't* is a contraction of "do not," *doesn't* of "does not." The proper contraction of "is not" is *isn't;* of "are not," *aren't.* *Daresn't,* if used at all, should be used only when "dares not" might be substituted. *Ain't* is a gross vulgarism.

EXERCISE XLII.

Insert the proper contraction (doesn't, don't) in each of the blank places:—

1. It — seem possible.
2. The captain — know what it is to be afraid.
3. John says he — understand the problem on page 266.
4. Why — she come?
5. — it seem strange that they — come?
6. Waldo — improve in penmanship as fast as he should.
7. It — look like pure water.
8. Why — he answer?
9. The boy will fail, but he — seem to care much.

May (might) or can (could).[2]—*Can* and *could,* which denote "ability" or "possibility," are often wrongly used in the place of *may* and *might,* which are the proper words to denote "permission."

EXERCISE XLIII.

Fill the blanks with the right words:—

1. — I leave the room?
2. You — go to the concert, but I doubt whether you — get a seat.
3. — we by searching find out God?

[1] "Foundations," pp. 81–82.   [2] Ibid., pp. 82–83.

4. — I have some more lemonade ?

5. — I have another piece of cake ?

6. — you tell me which is Mr. Ames's house ?

7. Mother says I — invite the girls to tea.

8. A man who knows himself to be right — afford to await the judgment of posterity.

9. — I write at your desk ?

10. You — come to see me whenever you — find time.

11. They asked whether they — have a holiday.

12. They were wondering whether they — be recognized in their disguises.

13. — I have the use of your sled ?

14. — I trouble you to get me a glass of water ?

Will or shall.[1]—Some grammarians teach that the future tense of "go" is: "I *shall* or *will* go," "You *shall* or *will* go," "He *shall* or *will* go," etc. The fact seems to be that there is only one form for the future; the other form, often given as an alternative, expresses something more than futurity, and is somewhat like a distinct mode.

A help to the proper use of *shall* and *will* is found in the original meaning of the words. At first *shall* and *will* were notional verbs,[2] *shall* meaning "to owe," "to be obliged," and *will* meaning "to wish :" as, "That faith I *shall* (owe) to God."[3] At present *shall* and *will* often retain some trace of their original meaning, *will* implying a reference to the will of the subject, and *shall* implying obligation or compulsion : as, "I *will* follow him to the end ;" "He *shall* be brought to justice ;" sometimes they are mere auxiliaries, with no trace of their original meaning: as, "It *will* rain to-day ;" "I *shall* be glad."

---

[1] "Foundations," pp. 83–88.

[2] By "notional verb" is meant a verb that has some distinct idea or notion of its own : as, "I *have* a ball." Here "have" expresses the idea of possession. In the sentence "I *have* lost my ball," the word "have" does not express a distinct idea ; it only helps to form a tense of the verb "lose": that is, it is not notional, but auxiliary.   [3] Chaucer.

For practical purposes the distinction between *shall* and *will* may be exhibited as follows :—

I. IN INDEPENDENT SENTENCES.

Simple Futurity.	*Volition,* implying that the matter is within the control of the speaker.
I (we) *shall* ⎫	I (we) *will* ⎫
you *will* [1] ⎬ go.	you *shall* [2] ⎬ go.
he (they) *will* ⎭	he (they) *shall* [2] ⎭

II. IN DEPENDENT SENTENCES.

In noun clauses introduced by "that" and depending on such verbs as "say," "fear," "think," etc., when the noun clause and the principal clause have different subjects, the distinction between *shall* and *will* is the same as in independent sentences. When the noun clause and the principal clause have the same subject, and in all other dependent clauses (introduced by "when," "if," "although," etc.), *shall* is in all persons the proper auxiliary to express simple futurity ; *will* in all persons implies an exercise of will on the part of the subject of the clause : as,

Different subjects : My sister says (that) Dorothy *will* be glad to go with us. (Futurity.)

My sister says (that) Dorothy *shall* not be left behind. (Volition.)

Same subject : Dorothy says (that) she *shall* be glad to go with us. (Futurity.)

Dorothy says (that) she *will* meet us at the corner. (Volition.)

Other dependent clauses : When He *shall* appear we shall be like Him. (Futurity.)

If she *will* come, we will try to make her visit pleasant. (Volition.)

[1] Sometimes used in a courteous command to a subordinate officer.

[2] Also used in speaking of what is destined to take place, or of what is willed by some ruling power.

4

III. IN QUESTIONS.

In the *first person* " will " is never proper, except when it repeats a question asked by another person. " Will I go?" would mean, " Is it my intention to go?"—a useless question, since the speaker must know his own will without asking.

In the *second and third persons* the auxiliary which is expected in the answer should be used.

> Will you dine with me to-morrow?   I will.   (Volition.)
> Shall you be glad to come?   I shall.   (Futurity.)
> Will your brother be there, too?   He will.   (Futurity.)

Would or should.[1]—"*Should* and *would* follow the same rules as *shall* and *will*, but they have in addition certain meanings peculiarly their own.

"*Should* is sometimes used in its original sense of 'ought,' as in 'You should not do that.'

"*Would* is sometimes used to signify habitual action, as in 'The 'Squire would sometimes fall asleep in the most pathetic part of my sermon;' and to express a wish, as, 'Would God I had died for thee, O Absalom, my son, my son!'"[2]

EXERCISE XLIV.

Distinguish in meaning between the following sentences:—

1. I will (shall) meet you in the village.
2. I will (shall) be obeyed.
3. Will he come?   Shall he come?
4. You will (shall) repent of this.
5. He will (shall) not see me.
6. You will (shall) have a new suit to-morrow.
7. Shall (will) you stay at home to-night?
8. We will (shall) not be left alone.
9. She will (shall) have a reward if she continues faithful.

[1] "Foundations," pp. 88–90.
[2] A. S. Hill: Principles of Rhetoric, revised edition, p. 63.

10. He would (should) start in spite of the danger.
11. Shall (will) you be a candidate?
12. He said he would (should) not go.
13. I shall (will) never see him again.
14. You will (shall) know to-morrow the result of the examination.
15. Will (shall) he who fails be allowed to try again?
16. Will (shall) the admission fee be twenty-five or fifty cents?
17. He thought there would (should) be a charge.
18. I will (shall) be the last to go.
19. He thought I would (should) wait.
20. He says that she will (shall) not eat watermelon.
21. If she disobeyed she would (should) be punished.
22. Do you think I should (would) go under the circumstances?
23. If they would (should) come, the danger would be averted.
24. If I would (should) say so, he would dislike me.
25. He says he will (shall) not come, since she forgot him at first.
26. We will (shall) come as soon as we can.
27. I will (shall) not endure his rudeness.
28. John says he will (shall) stay to see the game.

EXERCISE XLV.

Insert the proper auxiliary (will, shall) in each blank in the following sentences :—

1. I — be drowned; nobody — help me.
2. You — have a wet day for your journey.
3. He says he — not be able to come.
4. We — not soon forget this picnic.
5. He — repent of his folly when it is too late.
6. We — be pleased to have you call.
7. The gathering — be informal; therefore I — not need my dress suit.
8. We — have occasion to test the wires to-night.
9. I — be obliged to you for your autograph.
10. He — be obliged to you.
11. The managers have agreed that the race — be rowed again.
12. Do you think we — have rain?
13. If the fire is not put out soon, we — have the whole town to rebuild.

14. Do not fear; we — be all right.

15. A prize is offered to whoever — guess this conundrum.

16. We — find ourselves much mistaken.

17. The time is coming when we — have to go elsewhere for lumber.

18. Are you not afraid that you — miss the train?

19. Yes, I fear that I — miss the train.

20. He is afraid that he — miss the train.

21. They say I — find picture-galleries in every city.

22. Think what a happy life we — live.

23. If you will call for me, I — be glad to go with you.

24. I — be sixteen in May.

25. John thinks he — be sick to-morrow.

26. He says James — be sick to-morrow.

27. Howard thinks he — probably live to old age.

28. Howard thinks his brother — probably live to old age.

29. He tells me that he — be ten next month.

30. We — be all right if Congress will (shall) adjourn without tampering with the tariff.

31. If we examine the falling snow, we — find that each flake consists of particles of ice.

32. He has resolved that he — not answer the letter.

33. She has resolved that her daughter — not answer his letter.

34. I — feel greatly obliged if you — tell me.

35. When He — appear we — be like Him.

36. I hope we — be in time to get good seats.

37. When — I come to get my paper?

38. — I put more coal on the fire?

39. — you be sorry to leave Boston?

40. — you be elected?

41. When — we three meet again?

42. — I fetch a chair for you?

43. — you be surprised to hear it?

44. — you do me the favor to reply by return mail?

45. — we have time to get our tickets?

46. — you have time to get your ticket?

47. — he have time to get his ticket?

48. — there be time to get our tickets?

49. — you be at leisure after dinner?

50. — I find you at home?

51. When — we have peace ?
52. — he find gold there ? — we find any?
53. — we hear a good lecture if we go ?
54. If I fail on this examination, — I be allowed to take it over again ?

EXERCISE XLVI.

Insert the proper auxiliary (would, should) in each blank in the following sentences :—

1. I — like to know who he is.
2. We — prefer to go by boat from Rhinebeck.
3. He — prefer to go by boat from Poughkeepsie.
4. He — be sorry to miss his train.
5. I — be sorry to lose this umbrella.
6. I — feel hurt if he — abuse my hospitality in that way.
7. Were I to go, I — get tired.
8. He ought to have known that we — be ruined.
9. I — think he — know they are fooling him.
10. The head-master decided that you — be promoted.
11. Ralph said he — (volition) not stay at the hotel if it were not better kept.
12. Though I — die for it, yet — I do it.
13. I was afraid she — not come.
14. If I knew where she is, I — write to her.
15. We — have been paid, if the treasurer had been at home.
16. They — have been paid, if the treasurer had been at home.
17. I said nothing lest she — feel hurt.
18. I asked her whether she — come again.
19. He promised that it — not occur again.
20. If it — rain, we would not start.
21. Queen Isabella offered a reward to the first man who — discover land.
22. Cornelia was afraid that we.— miss the train.
23. I expected that they — accept the proposal.
24. He promised that it — not occur again.
25. Franklin resolved that Collins — row. Collins said that he — not row, but that Franklin — row in his place.
26. At first I did not think I — enjoy seeing the World's Fair.
27. What — we do without our friends ?
28. If he — come to-day, would (should) you be ready ?

Questions of Tense.[1]—The tense of a verb should correctly express the time referred to. Most errors in the use of tenses are violations of some one of the following principles, which are established by good usage:—

1. Principal verbs referring to the same time should be in the same tense.

2. The *perfect indicative* represents something as now completed—as begun in the past but continuing till the present, at least in its consequences: as, "I *have lost* my book" (so that now I do not have it); "This house *has stood* for ninety years" (it is still standing); "Bishop Brooks *has died*, but he *has left* us his example" (he is not now among us, but we have his example).

3. The tense of the verb in a dependent clause varies with the tense of the principal verb:[2] as,

> I *know* he *will* come.
> I *knew* he *would* come.
> I *have taken* the first train, that I *may* arrive early.
> I *had taken* the first train, that I *might* arrive early.
> Blanche *will be* frightened if she *sees* the bat.
> Blanche *would be* frightened if she *saw* the bat.
> Blanche *would have been* frightened if she *had seen* the bat.

Present facts and unchangeable truths, however, should be expressed in the present tense, regardless of the tense of the principal verb: as, "What did you say his name *is?*"

4. The *perfect infinitive* is properly used to denote action which is completed at the time denoted by the principal verb: as, "I am glad *to have seen* Niagara Falls;" "He felt sorry *to have hurt* your feelings."

EXCEPTION. — *Ought, must, need,* and *should* (in the sense of "ought") have no distinctive form to denote past time; with these verbs present

[1] "Foundations," pp. 93–98.
[2] This is sometimes called the "Law of the Sequence of Tenses."

time is denoted by putting the complementary infinitive in the present tense, past time is denoted by putting the complementary infinitive in the perfect tense: as, "You ought *to go*," "You ought *to have gone;*" "He should *be* careful," "He should *have been* careful." A similar change from the present to the perfect infinitive is found after *could* and *might* in some of their uses: as, "I could *go*," "I could *have gone;*" "You might *answer*," "You might *have answered.*"

EXERCISE XLVII.

Distinguish in meaning between the following:—

1. The house stood (has stood) twenty years.
2. The messenger came (has come).
3. He should stay (have stayed).
4. It rained (has rained) for two weeks.
5. He was believed to live (to have lived) a happy life.
6. He ought to go (to have gone).
7. He deposited (has deposited) the money in bank.
8. I am sure I could go (have gone) alone.
9. Yesterday at three o'clock I completed (had completed) my work.
10. He must be (have been) weary.
11. He appeared to be (have been) crying.
12. He need not go. He need not have gone.
13. The horse jumped (had jumped) into the field, and began (had begun) to eat the corn.
14. Achilles is said to be (have been) buried at the foot of this hill.

EXERCISE XLVIII.

Which of the italicized forms is right?—

1. Where did you say Pike's Peak *is* (*was*)?
2. I intended *to do* (*to have done*) it yesterday.
3. Atlas *is* (*was*) a mythical giant who was supposed *to hold* (*to have held*) the sky on his shoulders.
4. I do not think that any one would say that winter *is* (*was*) preferable to spring.
5. Cadmus was supposed *to build* (*to have built*) Thebes.
6. Your father grieves *to hear* (*to have heard*) of your bad conduct.
7. Would he have been willing *to go* (*to have gone*) with you?
8. I meant *to write* (*to have written*) yesterday.
9. He tried to learn how far it *is* (*was*) from New York to Syracuse.

10. He hardly knew that two and two *make* (*made*) four.

11. His experience proved that there *is* (*was*) many a slip 'twixt the cup and the lip.

12. Carrie knew that water *is* (*was*) composed of two gases.

13. It was their duty *to prevent* (*to have prevented*) this outrage.

14. He was reported *to rescue* (*to have rescued*) the drowning man.

15. It would have been unkind *to refuse* (*to have refused*) to *help* (*to have helped*) him.

16. It would not have been difficult *to prevent* (*to have prevented*) the disaster.

17. Where did you say Gettysburg *is* (*was*)?

18. It was as true as that he *is* (*was*) listening to me when I said it.

19. It was harder than I expected it would *be* (*have been*).

20. Homer is supposed *to be* (*to have been*) born about 850 B.C.

21. When I came I intended *to buy* (*to have bought*) all Paris.

22. Washington is known *to have* (*to have had*) many narrow escapes.

23. If you would only wait, your success *will* (*would*) be certain.

24. Is he very sick? I should say he *is* (*was*).

25. Who first asserted that virtue *is* (*was*) its own reward?

26. We have done no more than it was our duty *to do* (*to have done*).

27. What building *is* (*was*) that which we just passed?

28. He impressed on us the truth that honesty *is* (*was*) the best policy.

29. He expected *to see* (*to have seen*) you to-morrow.

30. He expected *to win* (*to have won*) the suit, and was astonished at the decision of the court.

31. The result of such constant reading by poor light would have been *to destroy* (*to have destroyed*) his sight.

32. It would have given me great satisfaction *to relieve* (*to have relieved*) him from his distress.

33. Who would have thought it possible *to receive* (*to have received*) a reply from India so soon?

34. It would have been better *to wait* (*to have waited*).

35. I should like *to hear* (*to have heard*) Daniel Webster's reply to Hayne.

36. The furniture was *to be* (*to have been*) sold at auction.

37. It was a pity I was the only child, for my mother had fondness of heart enough *to spoil* (*to have spoiled*) a dozen children.

38. I am writing to him so that he *may* (*might*) be ready for us.

39. I have written to him so that he *may* (*might*) be ready for us.

40. I wrote to him so that he *may* (*might*) be ready for us.

Examine the tenses in the following sentences, explain any errors which you find, and correct them :—

1. I knew him since boyhood.

2. It was a superstition among the Mexicans that a bullet will not kill a man unless it has his name stamped on it.

3. Being absent from the last recitation, I am unable to write on the subject assigned this morning.

4. Soon after Oliver reached home a servant announces the presence of Charles.

5. " 'Got any luck ?' says I. 'No,' says he. 'Well,' says I, 'I've got the finest string of trout ever was seen.' "

6. Be virtuous and you would be happy.

7. Stackhouse believed that he solved the problem he had so long studied over, and yesterday afternoon he started from his house, No. 2446 North Tenth Street, to make a test.

8. This beautiful little bird that appears to the king and tries to warn him, was not an ordinary bird.

9. Next September I shall be at school three years.

10. I know very little about the "Arabian Nights," for I have never read any of the stories before I came to this school.

11. If he received your instructions he would have obeyed them.

12. Before he was going to have the sign printed he submitted it to his friends for corrections.

13. The Balloon Society recently invited Mr. Gould to read before them a paper on yachting. Mr. Gould, in reply, has expressed regret that the shortness of his visit will prevent him from accepting the invitation.

14. I should be obliged to him if he will gratify me in that respect.

15. While he was in England the British had given him very honorable positions in America in order to have his help if they had any trouble with the colonies.

16. Up and down the engines pounded. It is a good twenty-one knots now, and the upper deck abaft the chart-house began rapidly to fill.

4*

17. Mr. and Mrs. Lincoln regret that a previous engagement will prevent them from accepting Mrs. Black's kind invitation for Thursday.

18. Mr. Rockwell will accept with pleasure the invitation of Mr. and Mrs. Pembroke for Tuesday evening, December 3d.

19. I am sure that he has been there and did what was required of him.

20. He might probably have been desirous, in the first place, to have dried his clothes and refreshed himself.

21. He could not have failed to have aroused suspicion.

22. When, on the return of Dr. Primrose's son Moses from the Fair, the family had discovered how he had been cheated, we are shown an admirable picture of home life.

23. Apart from his love, Orlando was also a noble youth. When old Adam, at last overcome by fatigue, sank in the footsteps of Orlando, Orlando tries to encourage and assist him.

24. The increase in tonnage was not so rapid as it would have been were it not for the Act of 1790.

Indicative or Subjunctive.[1]—The modern tendency to drop the subjunctive is unfortunate, for the distinction between the subjunctive and the indicative is too useful to be abandoned.[2]. A knowledge of the difference between these modes in English is especially important in view of the difficulty which pupils complain of in mastering the uses of the Latin subjunctive or the Greek subjunctive and optative.[3] For these reasons more space is given to the subjunctive in this book than would be called for by a mere discussion of modern English usage.

[1] "Foundations," pp. 98–101.

[2] "Some people seem to think that the subjunctive mood is as good as lost, that it is doomed, and that its retention is hopeless. If its function were generally appreciated, it might even now be saved. . . . If we lose the Subjunctive Verb, it will certainly be a grievous impoverishment to our literary language, were it only for its value in giving variation to diction—and I make bold to assert that the writer who helps to keep it up deserves public gratitude."—John Earle: English Prose, its Elements, History, and Usage, p. 172.

[3] "The lecturer also put in a plea for more vitality in the teaching of

Forms of the Subjunctive.—In form the English subjunctive differs from the indicative in several ways :—

1. In the single case of the verb *to be* there are distinct forms for the present and past tenses, namely :—

Present.		Past.	
I, we		I *were*, we	
thou, you	} *be.*	thou *wert*, you	} *were.*
he, they		he *were*, they	

EXAMPLES.—"See that my room *be*[1] got ready at once." "I will work you a banner if you *be*[1] victorious." "The headsman feels if the axe *be*[1] sharp." "Take care lest you *be* deceived." "Judge not that ye *be* not judged." "I will beard them, though they *be*[1] more fanged than wolves and bears." "If I *were* you, I would not say that." "If you *were* more studious, you would rank high." "Would that my parents *were* here!"

2. In *other verbs* the subjunctive form is distinguishable from the indicative in the second and third persons singular by the absence of the personal endings *-th*, *-s*, or *-st :* as,

Present Indicative : I have, thou hast, he has (hath).
   Subjunctive : I have, thou have, he have.
Past Indicative : I had, thou hadst, he had.
   Subjunctive : I had, thou had, he had.

Present Indicative : I come, thou comest, he comes (cometh).
  Subjunctive : I come, thou come, he come.
Past Indicative : I came, thou camest, he came.
  Subjunctive : I came, thou came, he came.

English, which ought to be made the gate to other languages. Many of the difficult questions of Latin syntax might be examined in the field of English, if only we were careful to treat our English critically. Whereas most grammars cut the ground from under them by denying the existence of a Subjunctive Mood. Until teachers recognize generally that, in such a sentence as 'If he had done it, it had been better,' we have a Subjunctive in both clauses, and a sentence essentially different from 'If he had loved her before, he now adored her,' English must forfeit half its value, both as a mental discipline and as a means of approach to Latin, Greek, and German."—From a report of a Lecture by Prof. Sonnenschein, of the Mason College, quoted in Earle's "English Prose," p. 55.

[1] In such sentences the indicative would be, according to modern usage, correct, and it is more common.

EXAMPLES.—"Long *live* the king!" "If thou *go*, see that thou *offend* not." "It is better he *die*." "Though he *slay* me, yet will I trust him." "Unless he *behave*[1] better, he will be punished." "If I will that he *tarry*[1] till I come, what is that to thee?" "Govern well thy appetite, lest sin *surprise* thee." "If my sister *saw* this snake, she would be frightened." "I wish I *knew* where Charles is."

The perfect and pluperfect subjunctives are of course formed by means of the subjunctive present and past tenses of "have."

3. Very often, instead of the simple subjunctive forms, we use auxiliary verbs—*may* (past, *might*) and *would* or *should*—to express the subjunctive idea. "May" ("might") is common as an equivalent for the subjunctive mode in clauses denoting a purpose, a wish, a hope, or a fear: as, "Bring him the book, that he *may read* to us;" "*May* he *rest* in peace;" "I hope you *may succeed;*" "They were afraid we *might lose* the way." "Would" and "should" are common substitutes for all tenses of the subjunctive: as, "Walk carefully lest you (stumble) *should stumble;*" "If he (come) *should come*, he will find me at home;" "It (were) *would be* better if he (went) *should go* alone;" "If my sister had seen this mouse, she (had been) *would have been* frightened." In these sentences either the form in parenthesis or the italicized form is correct, though the latter is more common.

NOTE.—It does not follow that the verbs "may," "would," and "should" always express the subjunctive idea. In the following sentences, for instance, they express the indicative idea: "You *may* (*i.e.*, are permitted to) stay an hour;" "You *should* (*i.e.*, ought to) be punctual;" "Edith *would* not (*i.e.*, was unwilling to) come." In such sentences "may," "should," and "would" make simple statements of fact.

Uses of the Subjunctive.—The indicative form is used in expressing a fact or what is assumed to be a fact: as, "He *thinks* he *is* ill;" the subjunctive form indicates some

[1] In such sentences the indicative would be, according to modern usage, correct, and it is more common.

uncertainty or doubt in the speaker's mind: as, "Whether it *rain* or not, I will go."

The subjunctive idea occurs most frequently, perhaps, in *conditional sentences.* A conditional sentence is one that contains a condition or supposition. A supposition may refer to present, past, or future time. If it refers to present or past time, it may be viewed by the speaker as true, untrue, or as a mere supposition with nothing implied as to its truth; if it refers to the future, it may be viewed as either likely or unlikely. A supposition which is assumed to be true, or which is made without any hint as to its correctness, is expressed by the indicative. A supposition which is viewed by the speaker as untrue or unlikely is expressed by the subjunctive or a periphrase[1] for the subjunctive. When the character of the supposition makes the conclusion untrue or unlikely, the conclusion also is expressed by the subjunctive or a periphrase[1] for the subjunctive. The use of tenses is peculiar, as will be seen from the following table of a few common forms of conditional sentences. The tenses should be carefully noted :—

PRESENT.

If it *rains (is raining)* now, I am sorry.
Present indicative: A simple supposition without any hint as to its correctness.
If it *rained (were raining)*, I *should be* sorry.
Past subjunctive, both clauses: The speaker implies that it is not raining.

PAST.

If it *rained (was raining)*, I was sorry.
Past indicative: No suggestion of doubt.
If it *had rained*, I *should have been* sorry.
Past perfect subjunctive, both clauses: The speaker implies that it did not rain.

FUTURE.

If it *rains*, I shall be sorry.
Present indicative: The common, though inexact, form of a simple future supposition. [position.
If it *rain*, I shall be sorry.
Present subjunctive: Less common, but more exact. The future is uncertain.
If it *should (were to) rain*, I *should be* sorry.
Subjunctive, both clauses: The uncertainty is emphasized by the auxiliary form; the chances of rain seem more remote.

[1] See paragraph 3, page 84. The forms in "would" and "should" in conditional sentences, though they express the subjunctive idea, can hardly be called the "subjunctive mood." Sometimes they are called the "conditional mood."

Note 1.—When *if* is equivalent to "whenever," the condition is called "general," to distinguish it from "particular" conditions, which refer to some particular act at some particular time. General conditions always take the indicative: as, "If (whenever) it *rains*, I stay at home."

Note 2.—Sometimes there is no "if," and then the verb or a part of the verb precedes the subject: as, "Were it raining, I should be sorry;" "Had it been raining, I should have been sorry."

Note 3.—In such sentences as "If thou hadst been here, my brother had not died," it may perhaps be questioned whether "had not died" is indicative, as in the Greek, or subjunctive, as in the Latin, idiom.

Note 4.—Clauses introduced by *though* and *unless* take the same forms as clauses introduced by *if*.

Wishes are naturally expressed in the subjunctive. The *present* subjunctive denotes a wish for the future: as, "Thy kingdom *come*." The *past* subjunctive denotes a wish for the present which is unfulfilled: as, "I wish I *were* a bird." The *past perfect* subjunctive denotes a wish contrary to a past fact: as, "I wish you *had been* there."

EXERCISE L.

Tell the time referred to in each of the following sentences, and whether the speaker regards the condition as true, untrue, or uncertain:—

1. If all men did their duty, there would be less misery in the world.

2. Had I heard of the affair sooner, this misfortune would not have happened.

3. Were it true, I would say so.

4. I would go with you if I could spare the time.

5. She could sing if she would.

6. If love be rough with you, be rough with love.

7. If all the year were playing holidays, to play would be as tedious as to work.

8. If thou warn the wicked, and he turn not from his wickedness, he shall die in his iniquity.

9. He brags as if he were of note.

10. If the natural course of this stream be obstructed, the water will make a new channel.

11. If the natural course of a stream is obstructed, the water will make a new channel.

12. If the book was in my library, some one must have borrowed it.
13. If he knows the way, he does not need a guide.
14. If he still wishes to go, he may take my horse.
15. Had he followed my advice, he would be rich.
16.　　　　Had she lived a twelvemonth more
　　　　　　She had not died to-day.
17. Though gods they were, as men they died.
18. Though the law is severe, we must obey it.
19. If the law be severe, we must change it.
20. Though the vase were made of steel, the servant would break it.
21. Though the vase was made of steel, the servant broke it.

EXERCISE LI.

Tell the difference in meaning between the italicized forms :—
1. If he *is* (*were*) studious, he *will* (*would*) excel.
2. If he *was* (*had been*) studious, he *excelled* (*would have excelled*).
3. Oh, that you *may be* (*were, had been*) blameless.
4. Though he *deceive* (*deceives*) me, yet will I trust him.
5. Though he deceived me, yet *will* (*would*) I trust him.
6. Though he *deceived* (*had deceived*) me, yet would I trust him.
7. Though the boy's coat *was* (*were*) made of silk, he *soiled* (*would soil*) it.

EXERCISE LII.

Which of the italicized forms is preferable? Give the reason :—
1. They act as if it *was* (*were*) possible to deceive us.
2. If I *was* (*were*) in his place, I would go.
3. I wish my mother *was* (*were*) here.
4. See that no one *is* (*be*) forgotten.
5. If this *is* (*be*) treason, make the most of it.
6. If it *rain* (*rains*), the work is delayed.
7. If it *rain* (*rains*), the work will be delayed.
8. Take care lest you *are* (*be*) carried away by your feelings.
9. If he *acquire* (*acquires*) riches, they may make him worldly.
10. I could jump across the stream if it *was* (*were*) necessary.
11. If to-morrow *is* (*be*) breezy, we will go sailing.
12. If my father *was* (*were*) here, he would enjoy this.
13. If she *was* (*were*) at the reception, I did not see her.
14. If he *speak* (*speaks*) only to display his talents, he is unworthy of attention.

15. I wish I *was* (*were*) at home.

16. Though this *seem* (*seems*) improbable, it is true.

17. I should be surprised if this marriage *take* (*took*, *will take*, *should take*) place.

18. If the book *was* (*were*) in my library, I would send it.

19. I will see that he *obey* (*obeys*) you.

20. If a man *smite* (*smites*) his servant and the servant *die* (*dies*), the man shall surely be put to death.

21. Though he *is* (*be*) poor and helpless now, you may rest assured that he will not remain so.

22. I wish I *was* (*were*) a musician.

23. Make haste lest your ardor *cool* (*cools*).

24. He will continue his course, though it *cost* (*costs*) him his life.

25. Though a liar *speak* (*speaks*) the truth, he will hardly be believed.

26. Govern well thy appetite, lest sin *surprise* (*surprises*) thee.

27. Though gold *is* (*be*) more precious than iron, iron is more useful than gold.

28. Whether he *go* (*goes*) or not, it is your duty to go.

29. If he *was* (*were*, *should be*) elected, it would be his ruin.

30. If a picture *is* (*be*) admired by none but painters, the picture is bad.

31. If one *went* (*should go*) unto them from the dead, they would repent.

32. If an animal of any kind *was* (*were*) kept shut up in a box, it would surely die.

33. They will not believe, though one *rose* (*rise*) from the dead.

34. Clerk wanted. It is indispensable that he *write* (*writes*) a good hand and *have* (*has*) some knowledge of book-keeping.

35. If the debtor *pay* (*pays*) the debt, he shall be discharged.

36. If my sister *go* (*goes*), which I think is doubtful, she will surely call for you.

37. The most glorious hero that ever desolated nations might have mouldered into oblivion *did* (*had*) not some historian *take* (*taken*) him into favor.

38. He will see his error if he *substitute* (*substitutes*) " that which " for " what."

39. Though Dorothy *is* (*be*) young, she is tall.

40. Unless he *take* (*takes*) better care of his health, his constitution will break down.

41. If I lend you my horse, I *shall* (*should*) have to borrow one myself.

42. I hope that if any of my readers *comes* (*come, should come*) to New Haven, he may find the city just as I have described it.

Singular or Plural.[1]—The following principles, established by good usage, writers or speakers are liable to forget:—

1. The expressions *each, every, many a, either,* and *neither* are singular.

2. When the subject consists of singular nouns or pronouns connected by *or, either—or,* or *neither—nor,* the verb must be singular.

3. Words joined to the subject by *with, together with, in addition to,* or *as well as,* are not a part of the grammatical subject, but are parenthetical, and therefore do not affect the number of the verb.

4. Since a relative pronoun has the number and person of its antecedent, a verb whose subject is a relative pronoun agrees in person and number with the antecedent of the relative.

5. "When the subject though plural in form is singular in sense, the verb should be singular; when the subject though singular in form is plural in sense, the verb should be plural:"[2] as, "'Gulliver's Travels' *was* written by Swift;" "Five hundred dollars *is* a large sum;" "Half of them *are* gone."

6. "A collective noun, when it refers to the collection as a whole, is singular in sense, and therefore requires a singular verb; when it refers to the individual persons or things of the collection, it is plural and requires a plural verb."[3]

---

[1] "Foundations," pp. 101–108.
[2] A. S. Hill: Principles of Rhetoric, revised edition, p. 56.
[3] Ibid., p. 57.

EXERCISE LIII.

Insert the proper form of the verb "to be" in each of the blank places:—

1. "Horses" — a common noun.

2. Such phenomena — very strange.

3. The ship with all her crew — lost.

4. No less than fifty dollars — paid for what was not worth twenty.

5. Homer, as well as Virgil, — once students (a student) on the banks of the Rhine.

6. The committee — divided in its (their) judgment.

7. The genii who — expected to be present — deaf to every call.

8. France was once divided into a number of kingdoms, each of which — ruled by a duke.

9. Sir Richard Steele lived in the reign of Queen Anne, when the tone of gentlemen's characters — very low.

10. Each man employed in this department — paid for his (their) work.

11. Mathematics — my hardest study.

12. There — once two boys who were so exactly alike in appearance that they could not be distinguished.

13. Each of the heads of the Chimera — able to spit fire.

14. The jury — eating dinner.

15. "Plutarch's Lives" — an interesting book.

16. One of the most beautiful features of Kennebunkport — the tremendous rocks all along the coast.

17. The richness of her arms and apparel — conspicuous in the foremost ranks.

18.   My robe and my integrity to heaven
               — all I dare now call my own.

19. Refreshing as springs in the desert to their long-languishing eyes — the sight of his white cravat and his boots of Parisian polish.

20. The "Arabian Nights" in complete form comprise (comprises) twenty volumes and — written by different men.

21. Fifty dollars a month — paid by the government to the widow of the colonel.

22. Ten minutes — spent in a writing exercise.

23. — either of you going to the village?

24. Our happiness or our sorrow — largely due to our own actions.

25. The guidance as well as the love of a mother — wanting.
26. Every one of these books — mine.
27. General Custer with his whole force — massacred by Indians.
28. Three times three — nine.
29. Nearly three hundred yards of the track — under water.
30. To admit the existence of God and then to refuse to worship him — inconsistent.
31. The ebb and flow of the tides — caused by the attraction of the moon.
32. Six dollars a week — all he earns.
33. Nine-tenths of his time — wasted.
34. Three quarts of oats — enough for a horse's meal.
35. "Tales of a Wayside Inn" — written by Longfellow.
36. The rest of the Republican ticket — elected.

EXERCISE LIV.

Which of the italicized forms is preferable?—

1. A variety of pleasing objects *charm* (*charms*) the eye.
2. Already a train or two *has* (*have*) come in.
3. Each day and each hour *bring* (*brings*) contrary blessings.
4. The Senate *has* (*have*) adjourned.
5. No monstrous height, or length, or breadth *appear* (*appears*).
6. I am the general who *command* (*commands*) you.
7. Many a captain with all his crew *has* (*have*) been lost at sea.
8. The jury *who* (*which*) *was* (*were*) out all night *has* (*have*) just returned a verdict.
9. He *dare* (*dares*) not touch a hair of Catiline.
10. The ambition and activity of this railroad *has* (*have*) done much towards the civilization of the world.
11. Thackeray's "English Humorists" *treat* (*treats*) not of the writings of the humorists so much as of their characters and lives.
12. Addison was one of the best writers that *has* (*have*) ever lived.
13. This is one of the books that *give* (*gives*) me pleasure.
14. Give me one of the books that *is* (*are*) lying on the table.
15. This is one of the most important questions that *has* (*have*) come up.
16. Nothing but vain and foolish pursuits *delight* (*delights*) some persons.
17. Six months' interest *is* (*are*) due.

18. You are not the first one that *has* (*have*) been deceived in that way.

19. My room is one of those that *overlook* (*overlooks*) the garden.

20. A committee *was* (*were*) appointed to investigate the matter.

21. The greater part of the audience *was* (*were*) pleased.

22. The public *is* (*are*) respectfully invited.

23. The jury *was* (*were*) not unanimous.

24. Generation after generation *pass* (*passes*) away.

25. A glimpse of gable roof and red chimneys *add* (*adds*) far more to the beauty of such a scene than could the grandest palace.

26. The society *hold* (*holds*) their (*its*) meetings weekly.

27. What *is* (*are*) the gender, the number, and the person of the following words?

28. He made one of the best speeches that *has* (*have*) been delivered before the school.

29. He is one of those persons who *is* (*are*) quick to take offence.

30. *This* (*these*) scanty data *is* (*are*) all we have.

31. If the meaning of these passages is not carefully explained, some of the congregation may think that Matthew or Paul *is* (*are*) guilty of some unorthodox opinions.

Misused Verbs. — See the remarks under "Misused Nouns."

I. A RESEMBLANCE IN SOUND MISLEADS.[1]

Accredit, credit.—"*To accredit* means 'to invest with credit or authority,' or 'to send with letters credential;' *to credit* means 'to believe,'"[2] or "to put to the credit of."

Arise, rise.—"The choice between these words was primarily, and still often is, a matter of rhythm [euphony]. The literal meanings, however, or those which seem literal, have become more associated with *rise*, and the consciously figurative with *arise :* as, he *rose* from the chair; the sun *rose;* the provinces *rose* in revolt: trouble *arose;* 'music *arose* with its voluptuous swell.'"[3]

Captivate, capture.—*To captivate* means "to fascinate"; *to capture*, "to take prisoner."

Depreciate, deprecate.—*To depreciate* means "to bring down in

---

[1] "Foundations," p. 109.

[2] A. S. Hill: Principles of Rhetoric, revised edition, p. 38.

[3] The Century Dictionary.

value," "to disparage;" *to deprecate* means "to argue earnestly against" or "to express regret for."

Impugn, impute.—*To impugn* means "to call in question;" *to impute* means "to ascribe to."

Loan, lend.—The use of *loan* as a verb is not sanctioned by good use. Properly the word is a noun. A *loan* is money which a person *lends*.

EXERCISE LV.

Tell the difference in meaning between—

1. The Amazon *captivated* (*captured*) our hero.

2. The king *depreciated* (*deprecated*) Napoleon's effort to raise a new army.

8. The readiness with which men *impute* (*impugn*) motives is much to be regretted.

EXERCISE LVI.

Insert the proper word in each blank, and give the reason for your choice:—

Accredit, credit.

1. Mr. Lowell was —ed as Minister Plenipotentiary to England.

2. These reasons will — his opinion.

8. He did not — the strange report.

4. The contribution of five dollars previously —ed to Mr. Williams came from Mr. Brown.

5. Mr. Sherman is well —ed as a writer on finance.

6. The bank has not —ed me with the interest on the deposit.

Arise, rise.

7. The court — at four o'clock.

8. At the discharge of a gun whole flocks of quail would —.

9. The idea of a reward did not — in his mind.

10. Most of these appalling accidents — from negligence.

11. The men — against their officers.

12. Other cases of mutiny may —.

Captivate, capture.

18. Her husband was —d in the battle of Gettysburg.

14. Mr. S. was —d by the young widow's beauty.

15. Let us attack them now and try to — the whole squad.

16. It is not merely what Chaucer has to say, but even more the agreeable way he has of saying it, that —s our attention and gives him an assured place in literature.

Depreciate, deprecate.

17. Financial panics are likely to follow a —d currency.

18. His purpose was —d by all who knew it.

19. Both parties — war.

20. It is natural for those who have not succeeded to — the work of those who have.

21. He —s his daughter's desire to earn her own living.

22. An injurious consequence of asceticism was a tendency to — the character and the position of woman.

Impugn, impute.

23. We cannot deny the conclusion of a proposition of Euclid without —ing the axioms which are the basis of its demonstration.

24. The gentleman —s my honesty.

25. The power of fortune is confessed only by the miserable, for the happy — all their success to prudence and merit.

26. Mr. X. is uncharitable; he always —s bad motives.

II. A RESEMBLANCE IN SENSE MISLEADS.[1]

Antagonize, oppose.—To *antagonize* means properly "to struggle against," "to oppose actively," or "to counteract." "In England, antagonizing forces must be of the same kind, but in the political phraseology of the United States a person may antagonize (*i.e.*, oppose) a measure."[2]

Calculate, intend.—To *calculate* means properly "to compute mathematically," or "to adjust or adapt" for something. In the sense of *intend* it is not in good use.

Carry, bring, fetch.—To *carry* means "to take along in going;" to *bring* means "to take along in coming;" to *fetch* means "to go, get, and bring."

Champion, support.—The word *champion* is very much overworked, being often used in the general sense of "support." It should be restricted to cases in which there is the idea of entering the lists as champion of a cause.

Claim, assert, allege, maintain, declare, affirm, state.—To *claim* means properly "to demand as one's own or one's due." It is often loosely used, especially in the United States, for "assert," "allege," "maintain," "declare," or "affirm." To *assert* is "to say or declare in the face of implied denial or doubt." To *allege* is "to assert with-

---

[1] "Foundations," pp. 110–114.   [2] Murray's Dictionary.

out proof." To *maintain* is "to uphold by argument." To *declare* is "to say publicly, clearly, or emphatically." To *affirm* is "to assert on one's reputation for knowledge or truthfulness." To *state*, which is also often misused in the sense of "say," "assert," "allege," "declare," or "affirm," means properly "to express formally and in detail;" it always implies detail. (See "Foundations," pp. 113, 114, and "Practical Exercises," p. 99.)

Confess, admit.—"*Admit*, in cases into which the idea of confession does not enter, is preferable to *confess*. On grounds of idiom, however, 'I must confess' and the parenthetical 'I confess' are exempt from the operation of this rule." [1]

Demand, ask.—*To demand* means "*to ask* for with authority or with insistence." The use of "demand" in the sense of "ask" is borrowed, possibly, from the French use of *demander*.

Hire, let, lease.—*To hire* means "to obtain the use of;" *to let*, "to give the use of." *To lease* means "to give the use of by lease." The owner of a house *leases* it; the person who occupies it *takes a lease* of it.

Learn, teach.—*Learn* means to "acquire" knowledge, not to "impart" it. In the latter sense the proper word is *teach*.

"I have more information to-day than I had before," said Mr. Sheehan. "This has learned you something," said Mr. Goff. "Oh no," replied Mr. Sheehan, "it has taught me something." [2]

Like, love.—*Like* and *love* differ greatly in strength or warmth, and may differ in kind. *Like* may be feeble and cool, and it never has the intensity of *love*. We may *like* or even *love* a person; we only *like* the most palatable kind of food. With an infinitive, *like* is the common word, *love* being appropriate only in the hyperbole of poetical or rhetorical feeling. [3]

Materialize, appear.—*To materialize* properly means "to make or to become physically perceptible:" as, "by means of letters we materialize our ideas and make them as lasting as ink and paper;" "the ideas of the sculptor materialize in marble."

Plead, argue.—See *plea, argument*, p. 29.

Stay, stop.—"*Stay*, as in 'At what hotel are you staying?' is preferable to *stop*, since *stop* also means 'to stop without staying.'" [4]

---

[1] A. S. Hill: Principles of Rhetoric, revised edition, p. 18.
[2] Newspaper report.   [3] See the Century Dictionary.
[4] A. S. Hill: Principles of Rhetoric, revised edition, p. 19.

Transpire, happen.—*To transpire* means properly "to escape from secrecy to notice," "to leak out;" it should not be used in the sense of *to happen*.

EXERCISE LVII.

Tell the difference in meaning between—

1. Please *bring* (*fetch*) a chair from the next room.
2. You had better *carry* (*bring*) an umbrella with you.
3. He *asserts* (*alleges, maintains, declares, affirms, says*) that he has been robbed.
4. Mr. A. *stated* (*declared*) his opinion.
5. He *admits* (*confesses*) the fault.
6. The grocer *asks for* (*demands*) his money.
7. He has *let* (*hired*) the boat for the afternoon.
8. We have *leased* (*taken a lease of*) the cottage.
9. He is *learning* (*teaching*) the alphabet.
10. Dorothy *likes* (*loves*) Helen.
11. Washington *stayed* (*stopped*) at this house on his way to Philadelphia.
12. It *transpired* (*happened*) that we disagreed.

EXERCISE LVIII.

Insert the proper word in each blank, and give the reason for your choice:—[1]

Antagonize, oppose.

1. Ex-Secretary Windom —d ex-Secretary Sherman's bill.
2. The body is balanced by an incessant shifting of the muscles, one group —ing the other.
3. I am too weak to — your cunning.

Calculate, intend.

4. To-morrow he —s to hunt the boar.
5. Bradley was able to — the velocity of light.
6. He —s to go.

Carry, fetch, bring.

7. Farmers — their potatoes to market.
8. What shall I — you from Paris?
9. Harry, please — a chair from the hall.
10. Go to the flock and — me two young lambs.

[1] In some of the sentences one verb or another is allowable, according to the meaning intended.

11. The Spartan was to — his shield home, or to be borne home on it.

12. When he dieth, he shall — nothing away.

Champion, support.

13. The Republican party —ed this measure.

14. He —ed the policy of the administration.

15. Gareth —ed the cause of Lynette in the combats with the craven knights.

Claim, assert, allege, maintain, declare, affirm, state, say.

16. The heavens — the glory of God.

17. Rhoda constantly —d that it was even so.

18. I have endeavored to — nothing but what I have good authority for.

19. Nay, if my Lord —d that black was white,
My word was this, your honour's in the right.

20. She —s her innocence in the strongest terms.

21. I will — what He hath done for my soul.

22. What if Nemesis — repayment?

23. It is not directly —d, but it seems to be implied.

24. That such a report existed in Claudian's time cannot now be —d.

25. Geologists — that before there were men on earth this immense gulf was a forest.

26. He fared on in haste to — his kingdom.

27. Will Mr. L. — his reasons for disagreeing with the rest of the committee?

28. He —s that he will not come.

29. Both sides — the victory.

30. There is another point which —s our attention.

31. He —d that he had been robbed by A., but he showed no proofs.

32. He —s that the thief attacked him on Third Street.

33. Please — all the particulars of the disaster.

34. The woman —s that she left Bangor Thursday night, and was put off the train at Hermon for not paying her fare.

Confess, admit.

35. He —s that his opponent is a good man.

36. I — that I spoke too hastily.

5

37. I — that John was a thief.
38. Every man must — that he has occasional fits of bad temper.
39. The problem, I —, is difficult.

Demand, ask.

40. He —s why I will not go with him.
41. The highwayman —ed their purses.
42.   The pound of flesh which I — of him
        I dearly bought; 'tis mine, and I will have it.
43. He —ed the way to Chester.

Hire, let, lease.

44. Boats to —; twenty-five cents an hour.
45. We will — our country-house during the winter.
46. — us some fair chamber for the night.
47. Bathing suits to —.

Like, love.

48. I — to go rowing.
49. He —s to talk of the days before the war.
50. All children — their mothers.
51. She —s her blue gown.
52. Don't you — strawberry short-cake ?
53.   A maid whom there were none to praise
        And very few to —.

Materialize, appear.

54. The representatives of the other colleges did not —.
55. His hopes have not —ed.

Stay, stop.

56. The King of Denmark —s there during the summer.
57. — a few moments longer.
58. She is very kind to ask me to — overnight.
59. I am very tired ; let us — here and rest.
60. I've been —ing with my mother for a week.

Transpire, happen, elapse.

61. After a considerable time had —d, he returned to the office.
62. Silas takes an interest in everything that —s.
63. Presently it —d that Henry Roscoe was the obstinate jury-man.
64. Many things have —d since the war was ended.

III. ADDITIONAL MISUSED VERBS.[1]

Accept, except.—*To accept* means "to take something offered;" *to except* means "to make an exception of."

Advertise, advise.—*To advertise* is "to announce to the public;" *to advise* is "to give counsel or information to a person."

Affect, effect.—*To affect* is "to act upon," "to influence;" *to effect* is "to bring about."

Alleviate, relieve.—*To alleviate* pain is "to lighten" it; *to relieve* it is to go further, and "to remove it in a large measure or altogether."

Allow, admit, think.—*Allow* properly means to "grant" or "permit," not to "admit," "think" or "intend."

Allude to, refer to, mention.—We *mention* a thing when we name it directly. We *refer* to it when we speak of it less directly. We *allude* to it when we refer to it in a delicate or slight way.

Argue, augur.—*To argue* is "to bring forward reasons;" *to augur* is "to foretell," "to forebode."

Compare with, compare to, contrast.—"Two things are *compared* in order to note the points of resemblance and difference between them; they are *contrasted* in order to note the points of difference only. When one thing is *compared to* another, it is to show that the first is like the second; when one thing is *compared with* another, it is to show either difference or similarity, especially difference."[2]

Construe, construct.—"*To construe* means 'to interpret,' 'to show the meaning;' *to construct* means 'to build:' we may *construe* a sentence as in translation, or *construct* it as in composition."[2]

Convince, convict.—"*To convince* is 'to satisfy the understanding;' *to convict*, 'to pronounce guilty.' 'The jury having been *convinced* of the prisoner's guilt, he was *convicted*.'"[2]

Detect, discriminate.—*To detect* is "to find out;" *to discriminate* is "to distinguish between."

Disclose, discover.—*To disclose* is "to uncover," "to reveal;" *to discover* is, in modern usage, "to find."

Dominate, domineer.—*To dominate* is "to rule;" *to domineer* is "to rule in an overbearing manner."

Drive, ride.—We go *driving* in carriages, *riding* in saddles. We *drive* behind horses, we *ride* on them.

---

[1] "Foundations," p. 115.   [2] The Century Dictionary.
[2] A. S. Hill: Principles of Rhetoric, revised edition, p. 38.

Eliminate, elicit.—*To eliminate* is "to remove," "to get rid of;" *to elicit* is "to draw out."

Estimate, esteem.—*To estimate* is "to judge the value of;" *to esteem* is "to set a high value on," especially of persons.

Expose, expound.—*To expose* is "to lay bare to view;" *to expound* is "to explain the meaning of."

Frighten.—*Frighten* is a transitive verb, and is used correctly in "The locomotive *frightened* the horse;" "The horse *was frightened* by the locomotive;" "The horse became *frightened*." It should not be used intransitively, as in the sentence "The horse *frightened* at the locomotive."

Inquire, investigate.—*To inquire* is "to ask for information;" *to investigate* is "to make a thorough examination."

Insure, secure.—*Secure*, in the sense of "to guard from danger," "to make safe," is preferable to *insure*, since *insure* also means "to guarantee indemnity for future loss or damage."

Let, leave.—*Let* means "to permit;" *leave*, "to let remain," or "to go away from."

Locate, find.—*Locate* properly means "to place in a particular position," or "to designate the site of," as of a new building or purchased lands; it does not mean *to find*.

Persuade, advise.— *To persuade* is "to induce," "to convince;" *to advise* is "to give counsel or information."

Predicate, predict.—*To predicate* is "to affirm as an attribute or quality;" *to predict* is "to foretell."

Prescribe, proscribe.—*To prescribe* is "to lay down as a rule or a remedy;" *to proscribe* is "to condemn to death or to loss of rights."

Purpose, propose.—"The verb *purpose*, in the sense of 'intend,' is preferable to *propose*, since *to propose* also means 'to offer for consideration:' the noun answering to the former is *purpose*; to the latter, *proposal* or *proposition*."[1]

Repulse, repel.—*Repulse* usually implies hostility; *repel* is a milder term. We *repulse* an enemy or an assailant; we *repel* an officious person or the unwelcome advances of a lover.

Start, begin, commence.—To *start* is "to set out" or "to set going," and is not followed by an infinitive. Before an infinitive, "begin" or "commence" is used. "*Begin* is preferred in ordinary use; *com*-

---

[1] A. S. Hill: Principles of Rhetoric, revised edition, p. 19.

mence has more formal associations with law and procedure, combat, divine service, and ceremonial."[1]

Suspect, expect, anticipate.—*To suspect* is "to mistrust," "to surmise." *Expect*, in the sense of "look forward to," is preferable to *anticipate*, since *anticipate* also means "take up, perform, or realize beforehand;" as, "Some real lives do actually *anticipate* the happiness of heaven."

EXERCISE LIX.

Tell the difference in meaning between—

1. I *accept* (*except*) him.
2. Telegraphic communication was *affected* (*effected*).
3. The medicine *alleviated* (*relieved*) her suffering.
4. He *alluded to* (*referred to, mentioned*) the battle of Gettysburg.
5. The first sentence was not well *construed* (*constructed*).
6. Mr. Fox was *convinced* (*convicted*).
7. Blanche of Devon *disclosed* (*discovered*) the treachery of Murdock.
8. We are going *riding* (*driving*) this afternoon.
9. He *rides* (*drives*) well.
10. I will *inquire about* (*investigate*) the business methods of the building association.
11. The furniture has been *secured* (*insured*).
12. *Let* (*leave*) me alone.
13. He *advised* (*persuaded*) me to have my life insured.
14. He *purposed* (*proposed*) to divide the class.
15. Did you *suspect* (*expect*) us?

EXERCISE LX.

Insert the proper word in each blank, and give the reason for your choice:—[2]

Accept, except.

1. Let us — the terms which they propose.
2. In saying that the Alexandrians have a bad character, I — a few persons.
3. Why did you not — the gift?
4. He was —ed from the general condemnation.
5. It gives me pleasure to — your invitation.

[1] Murray's Dictionary.

[2] In some of the sentences one verb or another is allowable, according to the meaning intended.

Advertise, advise.

6. The procession was —d to start at half-past two o'clock.

7. Under these circumstances we — total abstinence.

8. The merchants were —d of the risk.

9. When I return, I shall — you.

Affect, effect.

10. She was greatly —ed by the news.

11. When a man is hardened in crime, no fear can — him.

12. They sailed away without —ing their purpose.

13. What he planned, he —ed.

14. Bodily exercise indirectly —s all the organs of the body.

15. The loud crash —ed my hearing for a while.

16. Severe cold will — peach-trees.

17. The invention of the telephone was not —ed without great labor.

Alleviate, relieve.

18. Some fruits are excellent to — thirst.

19. He gave me an opiate to — my pain.

20. His charity went far to — the wants of the poor.

21. My cares were —ed by his friendship.

Allow, admit, think.

22. He —(ed) it would rain to-day.

23. He would not — her to come.

24. I — she will come.

25. He at last —s that I was right.

Allude to, refer to, mention.

26. A Latin inscription —ing (to) the name of the road is cut on the rock.

27. The people of the country, —ing (to) the whiteness of its foam, call the cascade "Sour-milk Falls."

28. I proceed to another affection of our nature which bears strong testimony to our being born for religion. I — (to) the emotion which leads us to revere what is higher than we.

29. He —s (to) enterprises which he cannot reveal but with the hazard of his life.

Argue, augur.

30. It —s ill for an army when there are dissensions at headquarters.

31. Not to know me —s yourself unknown.

32. E'en though vanquished he could — still.

Compare to, compare with, contrast.

33. The generosity of one person is most strongly felt when —d to (with) the meanness of another.

34. In Luke xv. the sinner is —d to (with) a sheep.

35. Solon —d the people to (with) the sea, and orators to (with) the winds; because the sea would be quiet if the winds did not trouble it.

36. It appears no unjust simile to — the affairs of this great continent to (with) the mechanism of a clock.

37. Goethe —s translators to (with) carriers who convey good wine to market, though it gets unaccountably watered by the way.

38. To — the goodness of God to (with) our rebellion will tend to make us humble and thankful.

39. He who —s his own condition to (with) that of others will see that he has many reasons to consider himself fortunate.

40. The treatment of the Indians by Penn may be —d to (with) the treatment of them by other colonists.

41. Burke —s the parks of a city to (with) the lungs of the body.

Construe, construct.

42. We might — his words in a bad sense.

43. How is this passage in Virgil to be —d ?

44. That sentence is obscure ; it is not well —d.

Convince, convict.

45. The jury, having been —d of the prisoner's guilt, —d him.

46. I hope you may succeed in —ing him of his error.

Detect, discriminate.

47. I cannot — the error in the account.

48. The chemist —d the presence of arsenic in the coffee.

Discover, disclose.

49. Events have —d the designs of the government.

50. We often — our mistakes when it is too late.

Dominate, domineer.

51. Three powers there are that — the world : Fraud, Force, and Right.

52. No true gentleman —s his servants.

Drive, ride.

53. While Mrs. A. and her children were —ing in the park the horses ran away and overturned the carriage.

54. Will you go —ing with me in my new pony-cart.

55. While —ing in the park Mr. C. was thrown from his horse.

Elicit, eliminate.

56. Discussion is a good way to — truth.

57. His bearing under the trying circumstances —d the approval of all high-minded men.

58. It is the duty of a statesman to try to — the worst elements of society and to retain the best.

59. Let us try to — the true facts from this mass of evidence.

Estimate, esteem.

60. I — him for his own sake.

61. Men do not — highly the virtues of their enemies.

62. The shell of the hawksbill turtle is much —d for making combs.

63. At what amount do you — the cost of the journey.

Expose, expound.

64. Daniel Webster —d the Constitution of the United States.

65. Daniel Webster —d the villany of the Knapps.

66. The text was well —d in the sermon.

67. It is the business of the police to — vice.

Insure, secure.

68. Will you — my factory against fire ?

69.   For woods before and hills behind
            — it both from rain and wind.

70. The cargoes of ocean steamers are generally fully —d.

71. The city is —d by strong fortifications.

72. How are we to — to labor its due honor ?

73. To enjoy the benefits which the liberty of the press —s, we must submit to the evils which it creates.

Investigate, inquire.

74. A committee was appointed to — the needs of the laboring classes.

75. I will — his name and rank.

76. Edison has been busy —ing the nature of electricity.

77. A commission was appointed to — the causes of the strike.

Let, leave.

78. Please — me take you to town.

79. We — that to the judgment of the umpire.

80. Pharaoh said, "I will — you go."

81. Why do you — your house go to ruin ?

82. Peace I — with you.

83. I will — you know my decision to-morrow.

84. Please — me out at the corner of Twenty-third Street.

85. — us free to act.

86. — go !

87. — the beggar in.

88. — us — him to himself.

89. He — the cat out of the bag.

Locate, find.

90. The missing man has at last been —d by the police in Kansas City.

91. The part of the city in which the mint is —d.

Persuade, advise.

92. Almost thou —st me to be a Christian.

93. I —d him to take a walk every day, but I could not — him to do it.

94. Columbus was —d to give up the thought of sailing westward in search of the Indies.

95. When in mid-ocean, Columbus was —d to alter his course.

Predicate, predict.

96. This very result was —d two years ago.

97. Ambition may be —d as the predominant trait in Napoleon's character.

98. He —s that the month of July will be rainy.

99. Disaster to the voyage was —d by the enemies of Columbus.

Prescribe, proscribe.

100. Sylla and Marius —d each other's adherents.

101. The doctor —d quinine in doses of four grains each.

102. It is easier to — principles of conduct than to follow them

103. The Puritans —d theatres.

104. The number of electors is —d by law.

Purpose, propose.

105. I don't — to let you escape so easily.

106. I — that we go boating.

107. We —d to go to-morrow, but I fear the rain will prevent us.

108. I — to work hard this year.

5*

109. Bassanio —d to pay the bond thrice over, but Shylock declined the offer, for he —d, if possible, to take Antonio's life.

Repulse, repel.

110. He gently —d their entreaties.

111. The charge of Pickett's troops at Gettysburg was —d.

Start, begin, commence.

112. Rosalind tells Orlando to — his courtship, and he wishes to — with a kiss.

113. The *Spectator* was —(d) by Steele.

114. We have —(d) Homer's "Iliad."

115. We have —(d) to find out our ignorance.

116. We — to feel that perhaps Darcy is not very bad, after all.

117. We —(d) in an omnibus at seven o'clock.

118. She has —(d) to study French.

119. Franklin's voyage was —(d) under unpleasant circumstances.

120. It —(d) to rain in torrents.

121. The play has —(d).

122. Hostilities have —(d).

123. The people of Philadelphia were so much pleased with Franklin's pavement that they —(d) paving all the streets.

Suspect, expect, anticipate.

124. I — that my grandfather was a wild lad.

125. I — great pleasure from our association in this work.

126. The burglars — that detectives are on their tracks, but they — to elude the officers by hiding in the country.

127. I was determined to — their fury by first falling into a passion myself.

128. I — that my father will come on a late train to-night.

129. I — that the rogue thinks himself safe from detection.

130. The death of the general is hourly —ed.

EXERCISE LXI.

Tell why the italicized words in the following sentences are misused, and substitute for them better expressions:—

1. The death of his son greatly *effected* him.

2. The Prince of Wales does not *propose* to send a challenge to the owner of the yacht Puritan.

3. He is *learning* me to ride a bicycle.

4. I cannot *predicate* what may hereafter happen.

5. Will you *loan* me your sled for this afternoon ?

6. It is even *stated* on the best of authority that the Minneapolis is capable of attaining a speed of twenty-four knots an hour, and of keeping it up.

7. Miss Duhe *claims* that the clairvoyant divulged many things that were known to her only.

8. It is evident that whatever *transpired* during the interview was informal and private.

9. There is little in the "Elegy" to *locate* the church-yard which is referred to.

10. He says he cannot *except* the invitation.

11. Is the Governor's wife *stopping* at the Springs Hotel ?

12. Dr. H.'s well-known views have led him to *champion* the cause of Dr. B.

13. I do not propose to *disrespect*[1] the Sabbath.

14. Macaulay says Voltaire *gestured*[1] like a monkey.

15. I *love* to see kittens play.

16. I *expect* he must have arrived last night.

17. I *calculate* it will rain soon.

18. This dry weather *argues* ill for the corn crop.

19. Mrs. Dennett broke open the door, and found a startling state of affairs. In the hallway her daughter Grace was lying prostrate, and seemed to be in an unconscious state. She *awoke* her daughter, who, after she had regained her senses, related what had *transpired*.

20. Elizabeth *allowed* that he had given a very rational account of it.

21. He *calculates* to go to-morrow morning.

22. The Abbe was beheaded, not *hung*.

23. I am looking for a fault which I cannot exactly *locate*.

24. James W. Reed, who mysteriously disappeared several weeks ago, has been *located* in England.

25. I *expect* you feel tired after your long walk.

26. The strike of the tailors, which it was *claimed* would *transpire* yesterday, failed to *materialize*.

27. Do you *allow* to go to town to-day ?

28. She tried to *locate* the places whence the sounds came.

29. Floods in all directions. Middle and New England States *enjoy* their annual freshets.[2]

30. I had hard work to *restrain*[1] from taking some.

---

[1] Consult a dictionary.　　　[2] Heading in a newspaper.

EXERCISE LXII.[1]

Illustrate by original sentences the proper use of each of these verbs :—
Allow, learn, leave, let, loan, locate, accede, accredit, credit, arise, rise, captivate, depreciate, deprecate, impugn, impute, like, love, antagonize, champion, calculate, bring, carry, fetch, claim, assert, allege, maintain, admit, confess, demand, hire, let, lease, materialize, plead, argue, state, stop, transpire, accept, except, advertise, advise, affect, effect, alleviate, relieve, augur, compare to, compare with, contrast, construe, construct, convince, convict, detect, discriminate, disclose, discover, dominate, domineer, drive, ride, eliminate, elicit, insure, secure, esteem, estimate, expose, expound, investigate, persuade, convince, predicate, predict, prescribe, proscribe, purpose, propose, repulse, start, suspect, expect, anticipate.

[1] See Note to Teacher, p. 151.

CHAPTER VI.

OF ADJECTIVES AND ADVERBS

AN ADJECTIVE is a word joined by way of description or limitation to a noun or a pronoun.

An ADVERB is a word joined by way of limitation or emphasis to a verb, an adjective, or another adverb.

Vulgarisms.[1]—Every educated person is expected to know the correct use of the following words :—

Good, well.—*Good* is an adjective; the adverb corresponding to it is *well*. We say, "He had a *good* sleep;" "He slept *well*." *Well* is sometimes an adjective, as in "You look *well*."

Likely, probably, like.—*Likely* is now used as an adjective only, except in the phrase "As *likely* as not;" the corresponding adverb is *probably*. We say, "He is *likely* to come;" "He will *probably* come." *Like* as an adjective means "similar," as, "Men of *like* excellence;" "He looks *like* his grandfather;" "He was a man of *like* passions as we are." In the sense of "in the same manner as" *like* is followed by a noun or a pronoun in the objective case, and is called by some an adverb, by others a preposition: as, "He talks *like* her."

Less, fewer, smaller.—*Less* refers to quantity, *fewer* to number, *smaller* to size.

Most, almost.—*Most* denotes "the greatest number, quantity, or degree." It is always superlative and never means "nearly," which is the proper meaning of *almost*. We say, "*Most* of the boys are here; the time has *almost* come."

Near, nearly.—*Near* is an adjective; the corresponding adverb is *nearly*.

Plenty is now in good use as a noun only, as "*Plenty* of corn and wine."[2] Shakespeare used the word as an adjective in "Reasons

1 "Foundations," pp. 118–120. 2 See page 32.

as *plenty* as blackberries," but this use is obsolete. The use of *plenty* as an adverb, as "The food is *plenty* good enough," is a vulgarism.

Some, somewhat, something.—*Some* is an adjective, as, "*Some* water;" "*Some* brighter clime." *Somewhat* is an adverb, as, "He is *somewhat* better." "Somewhat" is occasionally used as a noun, as, "*Somewhat* of doubt remains," but in this sense *something* is more common.

This, these; that, those.—*This* (plural *these*) and *that* (plural *those*) are the only adjectives in English that have distinct forms for the plural. A common mistake is to use the plural forms with singular collective nouns, as "kind," "class," "sort."

First, second, secondly, etc.—*First* is both adjective and adverb. *Second, third*, etc., are adjectives only; the corresponding adverbs are *secondly, thirdly*, etc. *Firstly* is a vulgarism.

Everywheres, illy, lesser, light-complected, muchly, nowhere near, unbeknown are not in reputable use.

EXERCISE LXIII.

Insert the proper word in each blank, and give the reason for your choice:—

Good, well.

1. George played — in the football game this afternoon ; he is a — runner.

2. She embroiders very —.

3. The draperies do not hang as — as I thought they would.

4. Your coat fits you very —.

5. He always behaves —.

6. This pen will not write —.

7. He did the work as — as I could expect.

8. This is a — picture ; the artist paints —.

9. Mr. A. is a — workman. See how — he has laid this hearth.

10. George writes —.

11. Charles does not look — to-day.

12. He says he does not feel —.

Likely, probably, like.

13. It became evident that the duke was not — to have his own way in the assembly.

14. There is a difference between what may possibly and what may — be done.

15. Just as — as not you will meet him on the road.

16. He is — to die of hunger.

17. He will — die of hunger.

18. It seems — that he will be elected.

19. — he will be elected.

20. Japan will — defeat China.

21. If a man does not care for himself, it is not — that he will care much for others.

22. They are as — as two peas.

23. Tell me who is married, and who is — to be.

24. This is a — story.

25. As — as not you love her yourself.

Less, fewer, smaller.

26. A proper fraction is — than a unit, because it expresses — parts than a unit contains.

27. I caught seven fish; Carl caught a — number.

28. Look for no — punishment than death.

29. I saw not — than twenty beggars to-day.

30. Rebellion is sometimes a — evil than endurance.

31. Not — than twelve banks in New York failed to-day.

32. We have — than a half a ton of coal left.

33. People who live in the country have — things to talk about than city people.

34. He received — good than he conferred.

35. I have — books than you.

36. There were — people there than I expected.

Most, almost.

37. I have — finished my lesson.

38. You will find me in my office — any day.

39. — men dread death.

40. We come here — every summer.

41. We have — done.

42. This wheat is — too thick.

43. Though I saw — everything else, I failed to see Hagenbeck's trained animals.

44. — everybody has imperfect eyes.

45. The old man's strength is — gone.

46. — boys like play.

47. It rains in some places — every day.

48. — all flowers are beautiful.

Near, nearly.

49. It isn't — finished yet.

50. We are — the end of the lesson.

51. I am — suffocated.

52. We are not — through our work.

53. He is not — so young as I.

54. I will answer you as — as I can remember.

55. We are — the end of the term; our school-days are — over.

56. Mr. Patterson came very — breaking the greatest record ever made in America.

Some, somewhat, something.

57. Thank you, I feel — better this morning.

58. — attempted, — done, has earned a night's repose.

59. He resembles his father —.

60. She felt — encouraged by this (these) news.

61. — evil beast hath devoured him.

62. He knows — of Arabic.

63. We came back — sooner than we intended.

64. If a man thinketh himself to be — when he is nothing, he deceiveth himself.

65. Dorothy looks — like her mother.

66. Yes, I'm — frightened, I admit.

67. It provoked me —.

68. A widow, — old, and very poor.

This, these: that, those.

69. You will always see — kind of man lounging in front of taverns.

70. Take up — ashes.

71. — pile of clothes is (are) to be carried to the laundry.

72. — kind of tree is (are) common in Pennsylvania.

73. — brass tongs cost three dollars.

74. — class will be graduated in June.

75. In New England there is not one country-house in fifty which has not its walls ornamented with half a score of poems of — sort.

76. How do you like — style of shoe?

77. Do you like — sort of pen?

78. — sort of person is always entertaining.

79. Look at — assortment of knives.

80. Beware of — kind of dog.

81. Problems of — sort are very easy to solve.

82. Young ladies should let — sort of thing alone.

First, second, secondly, etc.

83. I shall — show why we should worship God, and — explain how we should worship him.

84. Adam was formed —, then Eve.

85. Let us consider — what the young ruler desired; —, what he had; —, what he lacked.

86. My — proposition is that the measure is unnecessary; my —, that it is unjust; my —, that it is unconstitutional.

87. I will not lie; I will die —.

88. I like the old English ballads because, —, they are very quaint; —, they show the derivations of many of our words; and, —, they show different steps which our language has taken in becoming what it is.

Adjective or Adverb.[1]—Illiterate persons often forget that adjectives go with nouns and pronouns, but adverbs with verbs, adjectives, and adverbs. Even cultivated persons are sometimes in doubt whether to use an adjective or an adverb after certain verbs, as "grow," "look," "sound," "smell," "taste." If the added word applies to the subject of the verb, it should be an adjective; if to the verb, it should be an adverb. We say "We feel *warm*," when we mean that we are warm; we say "We feel *warmly* on this subject," when we mean that our feeling is warm. "As a rule, it is proper to use an adjective whenever some form of the verb 'to be' or 'to seem' may be substituted for the verb, an adverb when no such substitution can be made."[2] Thus, "He looked *angry;* he spoke *angrily.*" Sometimes we may use either adjective or adverb with no difference in meaning: as, "We were sitting *quiet* (*quietly*) round the fire."

Regarding the *form* of adverbs, ill-taught pupils often suppose that all words ending in "-ly" are adverbs, and

---

[1] "Foundations," pp. 120–123.   [2] Ibid., p. 121.

that all adverbs end in "-ly." A glance at the italicized words in the following expressions will remove this delusion : "Come *here;*" "*very* pretty;" "he *then* rose;" "lay it *lengthwise;*" "he fell *backward;*" "run *fast,*" "*now* it is done;" "a *friendly* Indian;" "a buzzing *fly.*" Though no comprehensive rule can be given for the form of adverbs, which must be learned for the most part by observation, it may be helpful to know that most "adjectives of quality," like *gentle, true,* take the suffix "-ly" to make a corresponding adverb; and that the comparative and superlative degrees of adverbs ending in "-ly" usually prefix *more* and *most.*

EXERCISE LXIV.

Which of the italicized words is correct?—

1. Write *careful* (*carefully*).
2. His teacher spoke *cold* (*coldly*) to him after she found he had acted *dishonorable* (*dishonorably*).
3. Speak *slow* (*slowly*) and *distinct* (*distinctly*).
4. He behaved *bad* (*badly*).
5. He is a *remarkable* (*remarkably*) good shot.
6. They were in a *terrible* (*terribly*) dangerous position.
7. I am only *tolerable* (*tolerably*) well, sir.
8. He acted very *different* (*differently*) from his brother.
9. It is discouraging to see how *bad* (*badly*) the affairs of our nation are sometimes managed.
10. He writes *plainer* (*more plainly*) than he once did.
11. You are *exceeding* (*exceedingly*) kind.
12. He struggled *manful* (*manfully*) against the waves.
13. You have been *wrong* (*wrongly*) informed.
14. *Sure* (*surely*) he is a fine gentleman.
15. She dresses *suitable* (*suitably*) to her station.
16. That part of the work was managed *easy* (*easily*) enough.
17. You behaved very *proper* (*properly*).
18. I can read *easier* (*more easily*) than I can write.
19. She knew her lesson *perfect* (*perfectly*) to-day.
20. I live *free* (*freely*) from care.
21. Lessons are *easiest* (*most easily*) learned in the morning.

22. Walk as *quiet* (*quietly*) as you can.

23. He acted *independent* (*independently*).

24. He spoke quite *decided* (*decidedly*).

25. We ought to value our privileges *higher* (*more highly*).

26. He was *ill* (*illy*) equipped for the journey.[1]

27. *Relative* (*relatively*) to its size, an ant is ten times stronger than a man.

28. That will *ill* (*illy*) accord with my notions.[1]

29. He is an *exceeding* (*exceedingly*) good boy.

30. One can *scarce* (*scarcely*) help smiling at the blindness of this critic.

31. I had studied grammar *previous* (*previously*) to his instructing me, but to no purpose.

EXERCISE LXV.

Distinguish between—

1. We found the way easy (easily).
2. The prunes are boiling soft (softly).
3. He appeared prompt (promptly).
4. It looks good (well).
5. We arrived safe (safely).

EXERCISE LXVI.

Which of the italicized words is preferable?   Give the reason:—

1. Velvet feels *smooth* (*smoothly*).
2. Clouds sail *slow* (*slowly*) through the air.
3. This carriage rides *easy* (*easily*).
4. How *sweet* (*sweetly*) these roses smell !
5. They felt very *bad* (*badly*) at being beaten.[2]
6. Your piano sounds *different* (*differently*) from ours.
7. The storm is raging *furious* (*furiously*).
8. This milk tastes *sour* (*sourly*).
9. The soldiers fought *gallant* (*gallantly*).
10. She looked *cold* (*coldly*) on his offer of marriage.
11. Ethel looks *sweet* (*sweetly*) in a white gown.
12. How *beautiful* (*beautifully*) the stars appear to-night !
13. This coat goes on *easy* (*easily*).
14. How *beautiful* (*beautifully*) Katharine looks this morning.

---

[1] See page 110.   [2] See "Foundations," p. 121.

15. Luther stood *firm* (*firmly*) in spite of abuse.

16. It looks *strange* (*strangely*) to see you here.

17. Deal *gentle* (*gently*) with them.

18. The cry sounded *shrill* (*shrilly*).

19. Larks sing *sweet* (*sweetly*).

20. He felt *awkward* (*awkwardly*) in the presence of ladies.

21. He has acted *strange* (*strangely*).

22. The water feels *warm* (*warmly*).

23. We feel *warm* (*warmly*) on that subject.

24. The dead warrior looked *fierce* (*fiercely*).

25. The wind blows very *cold* (*coldly*) to-day.

26. War clouds rolling *dun* (*dunly*).

27. The shutters are painted *green* (*greenly*).

28. She works *good* (*well*) and *neat* (*neatly*).

29. Protestants believe that the bread of the Lord's supper is not *real* (*really*) changed, but remains *real* (*really*) bread.

30. Homer says the blood of the gods is not *real* (*really*) blood, but only something like it.

31. *Real* (*really*) kings hide away their crowns in their wardrobes, and affect a plain and poor exterior.

Alone, only.—"In the Bible and earlier English *alone* is often used for the adverb *only*, but it is now becoming restricted to its own sense of 'solitary,' 'unaccompanied by other persons or things';"[1] as, "He rode all unarmed, and he rode all *alone.*" *Only* is both adjective and adverb.

EXERCISE LXVII.

Fill each blank with the proper word (" only,", "alone ") :—

1. She — of all the family had courage to go — into that darkened room.

2. These books are sold in sets —.

3. Man cannot live on bread —.

4. This fault — is enough to make her disagreeable.

5. By chance — did he escape the gallows.

6. Not — at Ephesus, but throughout all Asia, Paul persuaded many people.

[1] The Century Dictionary.

7. To be successful a school paper must be supported, not — with subscriptions, but also with contributions.

Omitted Adverbs.[1]—Adverbs necessary to the sense should not be omitted. This fault is especially common after *so*, *too*, and *very*—words which, as they express degree, properly qualify adjectives or adverbs, and not verbs or participles; also after *behave*, which, like the noun "behavior," requires a qualifying word to determine the meaning.

EXERCISE LXVIII.

Supply the omitted adverbs :—
1. He was very struck by what she said.
2. I wish you would behave.
3. The king was very dissatisfied with his wife.
4. I have too trusted to my own wild wants.
5. If you cannot behave yourself, you had better stay at home.
6. We are very pleased to see you.

Redundant Adjectives and **Adverbs.**[2]—A word that is not needed is said to be "redundant." Redundant expressions should be carefully avoided.

EXERCISE LXIX.

Strike out the useless adjectives and adverbs :—
1. From thence they marched twenty miles.
2. Which do you prefer most, apples or oranges ?
3. Whenever I meet him he always stops me.
4. Celia wished to accompany Rosalind ; therefore they both set out together.
5. The view from the top is simply beautiful.
6. Finally Rosalind disclosed her true identity.
7. The exercises are appointed for 2 P.M. to-morrow afternoon.
8. There are numerous mountain streams all throughout this region which abound in brook trout.
9. The central pith of the report is as follows.
10. Secluded and alone, he now partook of his solitary repast, which he entirely consumed.

[1] "Foundations," p. 123. [2] Ibid., pp. 123–125.

11. Out of the second term I took out the factor x.

12. Right in behind East Rock we have a beautiful lake.

13. When everything was all ready they started off.

14. He was a boy of eighteen years old.

15. If the ground is uneven they just level it off with a shovel.

16. Once the two twins were shipwrecked while on a sailing voyage.

17. The purple bird was once a royal king named Picus.

18. A large search-light will show a sail at a distance of three or four miles away.

19. Each of the provinces was ruled over by a duke.

20. When he returned he entered into the printing business.

21. He had a good chance to shift off the sky to the shoulders of Hercules.

22. The mud falls off from the wheels and makes the street dirty.

23. An old merchant of Syracuse, named Ægeon, had two twin sons.

24. He was almost universally admired and respected by all who knew him.

25. Pretty soon the man's hands began to get all blistered.

.26. Before you go you must first finish your work.

27. He did it equally as well as his friends.

28. It must be ten years ago since he left town.

29. Collect together all the fragments.

30. The play opens up with a scene in a forest.

31. He has the universal good-will of everybody.

32. Please raise up the window.

33. The story ends up happily.

34. They always entered school together every morning.

35. Out of the entire pack only two dogs remained.

36. He went away, but soon reappeared again.

37. A monstrous large snake crawled out from under the identical stone on which you are this very minute sitting.

38. I was deceived by false misrepresentations.

39. This question opened up the whole subject.

40. Let us, however, endeavor to trace up some of this hearsay evidence as far towards its source as we are able.

41. I will see you later on.

Misused Adjectives and Adverbs.'—See the remarks under "Misused Nouns." An amusing illustration of misused adjectives was furnished by an illiterate man who introduced his second wife to a friend as "My *late* wife."

I.

Aggravating, irritating.—In good use *aggravating* means "making heavier, more grave, worse in some way." It is often misused for *irritating, exasperating,* or *provoking.*

All, the whole.—See page 120.

Apt, likely, liable.—*Apt* implies a natural predisposition, an habitual tendency. "*Likely* implies a probability of whatever character; *liable,* an unpleasant probability."² One is *apt* to speak quickly, *likely* to hear good news, *liable* to be hurt.

Both, each, every.—*Both,* meaning "the two, and not merely one of them," groups objects, as, "*Both* were men of hot temper." *Each* means "all of any number, considered one by one," as, "*Each* boy recited in his turn." *Every* means "all of any number, considered as composing a group or class," as, "*Every* pupil should have a dictionary and use it freely." "*Every* directs attention chiefly to the totality, *each* chiefly to the individuals composing it. It may also be observed that *each* usually refers to a numerically definite group. . . . Thus, 'Each theory is open to objection' relates to an understood enumeration of theories, but 'Every theory is open to objection' refers to all theories that may exist."³

Many, much.—*Many* refers to number, *much* to quantity.

Mutual, common.—*Mutual* properly means "reciprocal," "interchanged." It is often misused for *common* in the sense of "belonging equally to both or all," especially in the phrase, "A *mutual* friend."

Partly, partially.—"*Partly,* in the sense of 'in part,' is preferable to *partially,* since *partially* also means 'with partiality.'"⁴

Quite, very.—*Quite* properly means "entirely"; in the sense of "very" or "to a considerable degree" it is not in good use.

So-as, as-as.—Both *so* and *as* are used as adverbs of degree correlative with the conjunction "as": unless there is a negative in the

---

¹ "Foundations," p. 125.   ² Ibid., p. 128.   ³ Murray's Dictionary.
⁴ A. S. Hill: Principles of Rhetoric, revised edition, p. 19.

clause *as* is generally used ; with a negative *so* is preferable to *as*. We say "It is *as* cold as ice," "It is not *so* good as it looks."

EXERCISE LXX.

Tell the difference in meaning between—

1. The circumstances of the offense are aggravating (exasperating).

2. She gave an orange to both (each) of them.

3. Each (every) man has his faults.

4. I had a call from both (each) of the boys.

5. He is apt (likely) to win the race.

6. A mutual (common) friendship.

7. The weekly reports are partially (partly) made out.

EXERCISE LXXI.

Insert the proper word in each blank :—

Aggravating, irritating.

1. Some of his remarks were —.

2. The prisoner said his wife's conduct had been very —.

3. He has an — manner.

4. He was too — by half.

5. The murder was committed under — circumstances.

All, the whole.

6. — (of) the boys were sent off at a day's notice to their homes. [For additional exercises, see page 125].

Apt, likely, liable.

7. An industrious man is — to succeed.

8. The ship was — to founder at any moment.

9. Bad books are — to corrupt the reader.

10. If a man does not care for himself, he is not — to care much for other people.

11. Youth is — to err.

12. Any kind of taxation is — to be looked on as a grievance.

13. We are constantly — to accidents.

14. Men are — to think well of themselves, their nation, their courage, and their strength.

Both, each, every.

15. — of them has (have) taken a different course.

16. — went his way.
17. He told me to invite — brother and sister.
18. He gave his hand to — of them.
19. In — cheek (cheeks) appears a pretty dimple.
20. I am feeling better in — way.
21. The oak and the elm have — a distinct character.
22. He'll be hanged yet, though — drop of water swear against it.
23. — soldier has a musket, and — one fires as fast as he can.
24. — inhabitant, male or female, young or old, was there.
25. In — ten women that the gods make, the devils mar five.
26. There is a row of beautiful elm-trees on — side(s) of the road.

Many, much.
27. We saw as — as twenty tramps.
28. He blames his uncle for — of his misfortune.
29. I found that — of the accidents on this railroad are caused by negligence.
30. How — of your peaches have you sold ?

Mutual, common.
31. Charles and his wife were happy in their — love.
32. They parted with — good feeling.
33. We have a — friend in Mr. Phelps.
34. I find, Miss Vernon, that we have some — friends.

Partly, partially.
35. Beware of acting —.
36. All men are — buried in the grave of custom.
37. This is — true.
38. The city of York is — surrounded by a wall.

Quite, very.
39. The country is — open.
40. The snow has — covered the ground.
41. Books — worthless are — harmless.
42. The island is — close to the mainland.
43. He was — dead when they found him.
44. You are — mistaken.
45. He is — ill.

So-as, as-as.
46. She is — amiable as she is beautiful.
47. He is — tall as his brother, but not — tall as I.
48. You have never — much as answered my letter.
6

49. Come — quickly as you can.

50. No other country suffered — much as England.

II.

Apparently, evidently, manifestly.—"*Apparently* is properly used of that which seems, but may not be, real; *evidently*, of that which both seems and is real."[1] *Manifestly* is stronger than *evidently*.

Average, ordinary.—*Average* implies an arithmetical computation ; if four persons lose respectively $10, $20, $30, and $40, the *average* loss is $25. The word is used figuratively by Dr. O. W. Holmes in "The *average* intellect of five hundred persons, taken as they come, is not very high." In the sense of "usual," "common in occurrence," "of the usual standard," *ordinary* is preferable to *average*.

Bound, determined.—*Bound* properly means "obliged," "fated," or "under necessity": as, "A man is *bound* by his word;" "We hold ourselves in gratitude *bound* to receive . . . all such persons." In the sense of "determined" *bound* is not in good use. In the sense of "sure" it is in colloquial, but not in literary, use.

Continual, continuous.—"*Continual* is used of frequently repeated acts, as, 'Continual dropping wears away a stone;' *continuous*, of uninterrupted action, as, 'the continuous flowing of a river.'"[2]

Deadly, deathly.—"*Deathly*, in the sense of 'resembling death,' as, 'She was deathly pale,' is preferable to *deadly*, since *deadly* also means 'inflicting death.'"[3]

Decided, decisive.—"A *decided* opinion is a strong opinion, which perhaps decides nothing; a *decisive* opinion settles the question at issue. A lawyer may have *decided* views on a case; the judgment of a court is *decisive*."[3]

Dumb, stupid.—*Dumb* properly means "mute," "silent." Its misuse for *stupid* is partly due, especially in Pennsylvania, to its resemblance to the German *dumm*.

Existing, extant.—That is *extant* which has escaped the ravages of time (used chiefly of books, manuscripts, etc.); that is *existing* which has existence.

Funny, odd.—*Funny* means "comical;" in the sense of "strange" or "odd" it is not in good use.

Healthy, healthful, wholesome.—That is *healthy* which is in good

---

[1] *A. S. Hill:* Principles of Rhetoric, revised edition, p. 39.
[2] *Ibid., p. 38.*   [3] Ibid., p. 18.

health ; that is *healthful* or *wholesome* which produces health. *Wholesome* commonly applies to food.

Human, humane.—*Human* denotes what pertains to man as man; as, "*human* nature," "*human* sacrifices." *Humane* means 'compassionate."

Latest, last.—*Latest*, like the word "late," contains a distinct reference to time ; that is *latest* which comes after all others in time : as, "The *latest* news ;" "The *latest* fashion." *Last*, which was originally a contraction of "latest," is now used without any distinct reference to time, and denotes that which comes after all others in space or in a series : as, "The *last* house on the street ;" "The *Last* of the Mohicans."

Lengthy, long.—*Lengthy* is said to have originated in the United States, but the earliest quotations found are from British authors. In the introduction to the second series of The Biglow Papers, Mr. Lowell wrote : "We have given back to England the excellent adjective *lengthy* . . . thus enabling their journalists to characterize our President's messages by a word civilly compromising between *long* and *tedious*, so as not to endanger the peace of the two countries by wounding our national sensitiveness to British criticism." *Lengthy* is used chiefly of discourses or writings, and implies tediousness. *Long* is used of anything that has length.

Mad, angry.—*Mad* means "insane ;" in the sense of "angry" it is not in good use.

New, novel.—That is *new* which is not old ; that is *novel* which is both new and strange.

Oral, verbal.—"*Oral*, in the sense of 'in spoken words,' is preferable to *verbal*, since *verbal* means 'in words' whether spoken or written." [1]

Pitiable, pitiful.—"*Pitiable*, in the sense of 'deserving pity,' is preferable to *pitiful*, since *pitiful* also means 'compassionate,' as, 'The Lord is very pitiful, and of tender mercy.'" [1]

Practicable, practical.—That is *practicable* which can be done ; that is *practical* which is not theoretical only : as, "a *practicable* plan," "a *practical* electrician."

Prominent, eminent.—*Prominent* means "conspicuous," "standing out so as to be easily seen ;" *eminent* means "distinguished in character or rank."

[1] A. S. Hill: Principles of Rhetoric, revised edition, p. 19.

Real, really, very.—*Real* is properly an adjective, meaning "not imaginary or counterfeit," as, "*real* diamonds." Its misuse for the adverbs *really* and *very*, as, "This is *real* pretty," is a vulgarism.

Scared, afraid.—The participle *scared* means "frightened;" *afraid* is an adjective meaning "in fear." Before "of," the proper word is *afraid:* as, "She is *afraid* of horses." *Scared of* is not in good use.

Grand, gorgeous, awful, splendid, elegant, lovely, magnificent.— *Grand* properly implies "grandeur;" *gorgeous*, "splendid colors;" *awful*, "awe;" *elegant*, "elegance;" *splendid*, "splendor;" *lovely*, "surpassing loveliness;" *magnificent*, "magnificence."

"We talk, sometimes, with people whose conversation would lead you to suppose that they had lived in a museum, where all the objects were monsters and extremes. . . . They use the superlative of grammar: 'most perfect,' 'most exquisite,' 'most horrible.' Like the French, they are enchanted, they are desolate, because you have got or have not got a shoestring or a wafer you happen to want—not perceiving that superlatives are diminutives and weaken. . . . All this comes of poverty. We are unskilful definers. From want of skill to convey quality, we hope to move admiration by quantity. Language should aim to describe the fact. . . . 'Tis very wearisome, this straining talk, these experiences all exquisite, intense, and tremendous." [1]

EXERCISE LXXII.

Tell the difference in meaning between—

1. The average (ordinary) yield of wheat.
2. He is bound (determined) to come.
3. There was continual (continuous) fighting for three days.
4. It was deadly (deathly) cold in the cave.
5. A decided (decisive) victory.
6. The boy is dumb (stupid).
7. His story is apparently (evidently, manifestly) true.
8. The existing (extant) portraits of Milton.
9. His actions were very funny (odd).
10. This is a healthy (wholesome) plant.
11. A human (humane) being.
12. His latest (last) attempt.
13. Long (lengthy) explanations.

[1] R. W. Emerson: The Superlative.

14. She became mad (angry).
15. A new (novel) style.
16. An oral (verbal) message.
17. A pitiable (pitiful) man.
18. Your purpose seems practical (practicable).
19. A prominent (an eminent) man.
20. He was really (very) glad to see us.

EXERCISE LXXIII.

Insert the proper word in each blank :—

Apparently, evidently, manifestly.

1. The motion which — belongs to the sun, really belongs to the earth.
2. The stranger was — in the prime of manhood.
3. The *apparent* (*evident*) discrepancy between the two narratives is not real.
4. Our country is — growing in wealth.
5. A straight line is — the shortest distance between two points.

Average, ordinary.

6. To be excited is not the — state of the mind.
7. This picture has only — merit.
8. — conversation is not instructive.
9. The — American is not wealthy.
10. The — expenses per man of the Yale class of '95 during Freshman year were $912.
11. The life of the — man is safer and more comfortable than it was a century ago.
12. The — age of the signers of the Declaration of Independence was nearly forty four.
13. Their — duties were easy.

Bound, determined.

14. He worked hard at his piece, for he was — to speak it well.
15. We have promised, therefore we are — to go.
16. I am — to win, if I can.
17. They were — that they would see the end of the play, even though they should miss their train.

Continual, Continuous.

18. He was exposed to — interruptions.
19. A — line in space.

20. — victory makes leaders insolent.

21. A — siege of six months.

22. The power of abstract study or of — thought is rare.

Deadly, deathly.

23. A — stillness.

24. The — bite of the rattlesnake.

25. My wound is —.

26. Her hands were — cold.

27. She, poor thing, was looking — pale.

28. Many savages have seen a musket kill small animals and yet have not known how — an instrument it is.

Decided, decisive.

29. He felt a — aversion to company.

30. Smith spoke out boldly in a — tone.

31. Creasy's "Fifteen — Battles of the World."

32. The nature of lightning was not known until Franklin made his — experiment.

Dumb, stupid.

33. A man who cannot write with wit on a proper subject is dull and —.

34. A deaf and — person.

35. I was struck — with astonishment.

36. Judging from his recitations, I should say that John is either lazy or —.

Extant, existing.

37. God created all — things.

38. Only two authentic portraits of Shakespeare are —.

39. There are — seven hundred and sixty-five of Cicero's letters.

40. Every citizen should exert himself to remove — evils.

Funny, odd.

41. It is — he never told me of his marriage.

42. He made the boys laugh by drawing — pictures on his slate.

43. You must have thought it — we didn't send for you.

44. He amused us with — stories.

Healthy, healthful, wholesome.

45. Tomatoes are said to be a very — food.

46. If a — body contributes to the health of the mind, so also a — mind keeps the body well.

47. Gardening is a — recreation for a man of study or business.

48. — food in a — climate makes a — man.

49. A — situation. A — constitution. — diet.

Human, humane.

50. A — disposition is not cruel.

51. To err is —; to forgive, divine.

52. In the time of Abraham — sacrifices were common among his heathen neighbors.

53. The Society for the Prevention of Cruelty to Animals is a — organization.

Latest, last.

54. The — men in the procession.

55. The — news.

56. The — of the Incas.

57. Have you read the — novel ?

58. The — foot-ball game of the season will be played with the Yale Freshmen.

Lengthy, long.

59. Cotton Mather wrote many — dissertations.

60. It is a — ride from Ellen's Isle to Stirling.

61. A — line of ancestors.

62. We were wearied by his — explanations.

Mad, angry.

63. His sarcastic manner makes me —.

64. That is nothing to get — at.

65.   I have heard my grandsire say full oft,
    Extremity of griefs would make men —.

New, novel.

66. We have a — horse.

67. A — feature of the entertainment was the "Broom Drill."

68. At the World's Fair we saw many — sights, especially in the Midway Plaisance.

69. Alice had many — experiences in Wonder Land.

Oral, verbal.

70. Some slight — changes have been made in the new edition of this book.

71. Were your instructions — or written.

Pitiable, pitiful.

72. The condition of the poor in our great cities is —.

73.   Be gentle unto griefs and needs,
    Be — as woman should.

74. The wretched girl was in a — plight.

75. A — sight.

Practicable, practical.

76. We have hired a — gardener.

77. This plan of campaign is not —.

78. We found the road not — because of the heavy rains.

79. A victory may be a — defeat.

Prominent, eminent.

80. Censure is the tax a man pays to the public for being —.

81. The figure of a man is — in the picture.

82. Frogs have — eyes.

83. Washington was a (an) — man.

84. John Quincy Adams was the — son of a (an) — father.

Real, really, very.

85. She came home looking — well after her long visit.

86. Protestants believe that the bread of the Lord's supper is not — changed, but remains — bread.

87. Homer tells us that the blood of the gods is not — blood, but only something like it.

88. I am — glad you have come.

89. He is — dead.

90. It was — kind in you to send me flowers.

91. Yes, I am — old; I am sixty.

92. He speaks — well, doesn't he?

93. — kings hide away their crowns in their wardrobes, and affect a plain and poor exterior.

94. This is — pretty.

95. We came on a — fast train.

96. She seemed — glad to see us.

97. The hotel is situated — near the sea.

Scared, afraid.

98. She was badly — when her horse ran away.

99. Harry is — of tramps.

100. Helen was — of the cows in the meadow.

EXERCISE LXXIV.[1]

Illustrate by original sentences the correct use of each of these words: —Both, each, every, aggravating, liable, likely, apt, mutual, partially, quite, average, bound, continual, continuous, deadly, deathly, decided, decisive, dumb, apparently, evidently, extant, funny, healthy,

[1] See note To the Teacher, p. 42.

healthful, wholesome, human, humane, latest, last, lengthy, mad, novel, verbal, pitiable, pitiful, practicable, practical, prominent, eminent, real, really, scared, grand, gorgeous, awful, splendid, elegant, lovely, magnificent.

Use of the Comparative and Superlative.—The comparative degree is preferable when two things or sets of things are compared, the superlative when three or more are compared.

To say "Iron is more useful than *any* metal" is clearly incorrect, because iron is included in "any metal," and of course iron is not more useful than itself. We must in thought set iron off in a class by itself, which we can do by inserting "other" after "any." "Iron is more useful than *any other* metal" is correct. After comparatives accompanied by "than," the words "any" and "all" should be followed by "other."

To say "Iron is the most useful of *any* (or, *any other*) metal" is also clearly incorrect, because we mean that iron is the most useful, not of. "one metal (no matter which)" or of "some metals (no matter which)," but of all metals. We should therefore omit the word "any," saying simply "Iron is the most useful of (all) metals." It is also incorrect to say "Iron is the most useful of all *other* metals," for iron is not one of the "other metals." Beware of using "any" or "other" with superlatives followed by "of."

EXERCISE LXXV.

Which of the italicized forms is preferable?—

1. Of London and Paris, London is the *wealthier* (*wealthiest*).

2. Of two evils, choose the *less* (*least*).

3. The *older* (*oldest*) of the three boys was sent to college.

4. Which can run the *faster* (*fastest*), your horse or mine?

5. Of the two Latin poets, Virgil and Horace, the *first* (*former*) is the *better* (*best*) known.

6*

6. Which is the *better* (*best*) of the two ?

7. Which is the *farther* (*farthest*) east, Boston, New York, or Philadelphia ?

8. There is no doubt about *him* (*his*) being the *better* (*best*) in the little group of friends.

9. Which is the *larger* (*largest*) number, the minuend or the subtrahend ?

EXERCISE LXXVI.

Explain and correct the errors in the following sentences :—

1. This picture is, of all others, the one I like best.

2. This engraving of mine I like better than any picture I have.

3. London is more crowded than any city in Great Britain.

4. London is the most crowded of any city in Great Britain.

5. She of all other girls ought to be the last to complain.

6. Our grammar lessons are the hardest of any we have.

7. St. Peter's is larger than any church in the world.

8. St. Peter's is the largest of any church in the world.

9. Noah and his family outlived all the people who lived before the flood.

10. Solomon was wiser than all men.

11. This State exports more cotton than all the states.

12. A cowboy is the most picturesque of any men.

13. Tabby has the worst temper of any cat I know.

14. He thinks Gettysburg has the prettiest girls of any town of its size.

15. The proposed methods of Mr. F. G. Jackson, the English arctic explorer, appears to be the most practical and business-like of any yet undertaken for exploring the polar regions.

EXERCISE LXXVII.

Construct sentences comparing the following things, using first a comparative, then a superlative form :—

1. The large population of China ; the smaller populations of other countries.

EXAMPLE.—China has a larger population than any other country. Of all countries, China has the largest population in the world.

2. John, who is very mischievous ; other boys, who are less mischievous.

3. Eve, who was exceedingly fair; her daughters (female descendants), who are less fair.

4. Smith, the best athlete; the other boys in the school.

5. Mary's recitations; the poorer recitations of her classmates.

6. The population of London; the population of the other cities in the world.

7. The circulation of the "Star;" the smaller circulation of other newspapers in the county.

8. Ethel's eyes; the eyes of her playmates, which are not so bright.

9. The examination papers of Professor A.; the easier papers set by other teachers.

10. Philip; his classmates, who are less bright.

11. Solomon, the wisest king; other kings.

12. Samson, the strongest man; other men.

13. Jacob's love for Joseph; his love for his other children.

14. Youth; the other periods of life, which are less important.

15. Demosthenes; the other and inferior orators of Greece.

16. The books read by Fannie; the fewer books read by her classmates.

17. This shady grove: other groves I know, which are less shady.

18. The reign of Louis XIV.; the shorter reigns of other French kings.

19. Shakespeare; other English poets, all of whom are inferior to him.

20. The Falls of Niagara; other falls in the United States.

Adjectives and **Adverbs incapable of Comparison.**[1]— Some adjectives and adverbs have meanings which do not vary in degree: as, *dead, perfect, wooden.* Such adjectives cannot properly be compared or modified by the words "more," "most," "so," "too," and "very."

EXERCISE LXXVIII.

Which of the following adjectives and adverbs do not vary in degree?—

Absolutely, brave, cloudless, cold, conclusively, continually, entirely, essentially, extreme, faultless, French, fundamental, golden,

[1] "Foundations," p. 135.

happy, impregnable, inaudible, incessant, incredible, indispensable, insatiate, inseparable, intangible, intolerable, invariable, long, masterly, round, sharp,. square, sufficient, unanimous, unbearable, unbounded, unerring, unique, universally, unparalleled, unprecedented.

Misplaced Adjectives and Adverbs.[1]—A word, a phrase, or a clause used as an adjective or an adverb should come next to the word, or words, which it modifies.

The word *only* requires special care. Observe how the position of *only* affects the meaning in the following sentences: "Only he lost his hat;" "He only lost his hat;" "He lost only his hat," or "He lost his hat only;" "He lost his only hat."

EXERCISE LXXIX.

Correct the errors of position in the following sentences:—

1. Metal reflectors are only used now for cheap search-lights.
2. I will only mention some of the best.
3. I only had time to read "King Lear."
4. He only spoke to me, not to you.
5. Coons are only killed with the help of dogs. The coon only comes out in the night-time.
6. Lost, a Scotch terrier, by a gentleman, with his ears cut close.
7. Canteens were issued to the soldiers with short necks.
8. We all went to the sea-shore for a little fresh air from the city.
9. At one time Franklin was seen bringing some paper to his printing-office from the place where he had purchased it in a wheelbarrow.
10. He went to Germany to patronize the people in the little German villages from which he came with his great wealth.
11. The three young men set out and finally arrived at the college dressed in girls' clothes.
12. The maskers were nearly dressed alike.
13. Erected to the memory of John Smith accidentally shot as a mark of affection by his brother.
14. Lost, an umbrella by a gentleman with an ivory head.
15. A piano for sale by a lady about to cross the channel in an oak case with carved legs.

[1] "Foundations," p. 136.

16. He blew out his brains after bidding his wife good-bye with a gun.

17. The Moor, seizing a bolster, full of rage and jealousy, smothered Desdemona.

18. Wanted, a handsome Shetland pony suitable for a child with a long mane and tail.

19. Wolsey left many buildings which he had begun at his death in an unfinished state.

20. My cousin caught a crab and took it home in a pail of water which we had for our tea.

21. I scarcely ever remember to have had a rougher walk.

Adverbs between **To** and **The Infinitive.**—"A careful writer will do well to avoid the construction which places the adverb between *to* and the infinitive. It is true that the construction is a common one; but it is also true that those who are most addicted to the practice are not those who count most as authorities on questions of good usage."[1]

EXERCISE LXXX.

Improve the arrangement in the following sentences :—

1. Hermes caused the milk pitcher of the old couple to never be empty.

2. His political enemies tried to in this way impeach the courage of the President.

3. He promises to earnestly try to do better.

4. To really know the man we must read his books.

5. Another project is to in some way modify the power of the House of Lords.

6. She dwelt upon what was comforting, though conscious that there was little to veritably console.

7. He proposed to either largely decrease the appropriation or to wholly do away with it.

[1] "Foundations," p. 140.

CHAPTER VII.

OF PREPOSITIONS

Misused Prepositions.[1]—A writer, in choosing the proper preposition to express his meaning, must rely chiefly on his sense of idiom, that is, his knowledge of English usage, but he may find the following notes helpful.

Among, between.—"*Among* is the proper word when the reference is to more than two persons or things, or groups of persons or things; *between*, when the reference is to two only."[2]

At, in.—Before names of places to denote "where," *at* is used when the place is so small as to be treated as a mere point, or when, although large, it is viewed as a mere point; *in* is used when it is desired to make prominent the idea "within the bounds of:" as, "He arrived *at* Liverpool in the morning and remained *in* that city two days." Before the name of the place in which the speaker dwells, if the place is of any size, *in* is generally preferred to *at*, unless the place is so remote that it dwindles in the mental vision to a point.

Back of.—*Back of*, though frequently heard in conversation and sometimes seen in print, is not in good use.

Beside, besides.—*Beside* means "by the side of;" *besides* is now used only in the sense of "in addition to," "other than:" as, "Who sits *beside* you?" "Who *besides* us knows this?"

By, with.—To introduce the agent of an action *by* is now commonly used; the material instrument or tool is usually introduced by *with:* as, "Duncan was murdered *by* Macbeth *with* a dagger."

Different from, different to.—*Different from* is preferable to *different to* and *different than.*

In, into.—"*In* implies presence inside of, or within; *into* implies movement to the inside of. Before a man can move *in* a room, he must already have moved *into* it."[3]

[1] "Foundations," pp. 142–148.   [2] Ibid., p. 143.   [3] Ibid., p. 145.

In, on.—Before names of streets, *in* implies some reference to surroundings; *on* is less definite, indicating location only.

On to, onto.—"Good use does not support either *on to* or *onto.*" [1]

Wait for, wait on.—*To wait for* means "to await," as, "We will *wait for* you at the corner." *To wait on* means "to attend on," as, "At dinner the women *waited on* the men."

EXERCISE LXXXI.

Insert the proper preposition in each blank:—

Among, between.

1. He divided the apples — the five boys.
2. There was a generous rivalry — the two friends.
3. I have no preference — many of Tennyson's poems.
4. There is bad feeling — China and Japan.
5. The money was divided — the six heirs.

At, in.

6. Napoleon died — Longwood, a villa on the island of St. Helena; Byron died — Missolonghi, — Greece.
7. Did he graduate — Oxford or — Cambridge ?
8. He is now — Ireland.
9. Milton was educated — Christ's College.
10. When shall we arrive — Rome ?
11. I am eager to visit a hundred places — Florence.
12. We live — New York.
13. Macaulay lived — London.

Beside, besides.

14. Have you nothing to tell us — what we have already heard ?
15. The boy stood — her.
16. — the large planets, there are hundreds of smaller planets called "asteroids."
17. Let me sit — you.

By, with.

18. The door was fastened — nails — the carpenter.
19. The Great Charter was signed — King John.
20. Thebes was founded — Cadmus.
21. Truth finds an easy entrance into the mind when she is introduced — Desire and attended — Pleasure.
22. He entertained us — a story.
23. He struck me — his cane.

[1] "Foundations," p. 146.

In, into.

24. The dog is — the water.
25. Come — the house.
26. Look — my desk.
27. Put more life — your speaking.
28. Throw it — the fire.
29. What put this idea — your head ?
30. Carry the basket — the kitchen.
31. She threw herself — a chair.

In, on.

32. The cable cars — Broadway.
33. Ellen and Harry are playing — the street.
34. The Murray Hill Hotel is — Fourth Avenue.
35. They carry on their business — William Street.

" With certain words good use requires special preposi-tions. Among these words are the following :—

abhorrence of.
absolve from.
accord with.
acquit of.
adapted to or for.
affinity between, to, or with.
agree with (a person).
agree to (a proposal).
averse from or to.
bestow upon.
change for (a thing).
change with (a person).
comply with.
confer on (= give to).
confer with (= talk with).
confide in (= trust in).
confide to (= intrust to).
conform to.
in conformity with or to.
convenient for or to.
conversant with.

correspond to or with (a thing).
correspond with (a person).
dependent on (but independent of).
derogatory to.
differ from (a person or thing).
differ from or with (in opinion).
disappointed of (what we cannot get).
disappointed in (what we have).
dissent from.
glad at or of.
involve in.
martyr for or to.
need of.
part from or with.
profit by.
reconcile to or with.
taste of (food).
taste for (art).
thirst for or after." [1]

[1] " Foundations," p. 148.

EXERCISE LXXXII.

I. *Tell the difference in meaning between—*
1. She confides in (to) her sister.
2. He differs from (with) me.
3. We are disappointed of (in) our guests.
4. He is in (*at*) New York.
5. He waited on (for) his mother.

II. *Tell what prepositions are required with these words:* Abhorrence, absolve, accord, acquit, adapted, affinity, agree, agreeable, averse, bestow, change (verb), comply, confer, confide, conform, in conformity, convenient, conversant, correspond, dependent, derogatory, differ, different, disappointed, dissent (verb), eager, exception, expert, glad, independent, involve, martyr, need (noun), part (verb), profit (verb), reconcile, taste (noun), thirst (noun), worthy.

EXERCISE LXXXIII.

Insert the proper preposition in each blank:—[1]
1. Please wait — me; I will come as soon as I can.
2. She married him — her father's consent.
3. The cathedral was rich — all kinds of golden vessels.
4. Moses received the laws — the people on Mount Sinai.
5. Evangeline died — Philadelphia.
6. — whom did they rent the house?
7. — whom can I rely?
8. The boy went in search — his sister.
9. The streams — this region abound — trout.
10. The traces of a struggle were seen — the tree.
11. They got — the carriage and rode away.
12. He has moved — New York, where he lives — an·elegant mansion.
13. He thought that he put the money — his pocket, but he found it — his shoe.
14. The paper was cut — small strips.
15. We stood — the landing.
16. The firemen went — the roof of the house.

[1] In this exercise the pupil must rely chiefly on his knowledge of English usage or on a dictionary. In some of the sentences more than one preposition is allowable, according to the sense.

17. He is down — the village.
18. What was the matter — him ?
19. He died — a fever.
20. When we were — Rome we stayed — a small hotel.
21. He lives — a frame house — Cambridge.
22. Her unladylike behavior gave occasion — many unpleasant remarks.
23. Caterpillars change — butterflies.
24. She lives — College Street, — No. 1009.
25. It was conducive — my comfort.
26. The calm was followed — a sudden storm.
27. The soil of Virginia is adapted — the production of hemp and tobacco.
28. The flower is excellently adapted — catching insects.
29. Congress consists — a Senate and a House of Representatives.
80. — what does happiness consist ?
81. — some sentences the conjunction is omitted.
82. A judge who has an interest in a case is disqualified — hearing it.
83. He was accused — robbery.
84. He died — starvation, she — pneumonia.
35. You may rely — what I say, and confide — my honesty.
36. The bird flew — the tree.
87. He let the knife fall — the creek.
38. What is my grief in comparison — that which she bears ?
89. Most persons feel an abhorrence — snakes.
40. He aspires — political distinction.
41. We were disappointed — the pleasure of seeing you.
42. There is need — great watchfulness.
43. I have been — New Orleans, and I am now going — New York.
44. We lived — a little village — the South.
45. I find no difficulty — keeping up with my class.
46. — every class of people selfishness prevails.
47. He divided his estate — his son, his daughter, and his nephew.
48. He is very different — his brother.
49. This was different — what I expected.
50. Compare your work — his, and you will see the difference.
51. My old yacht was small in comparison — this.
52. He is adapted — an out-door life.

53. His disobedience was attended — serious consequences.

54. His mother was overcome — grief.

55. We were accompanied — our parents.

56. A man should try to rid himself — prejudice.

57. He will profit — his experience.

58. The room was redolent — the perfume.

59. You must conform — the rules.

60. Fondness — horses was his leading trait.

61. We felt the need — some adviser.

62. I cannot reconcile this assertion — your other one.

63. Let us cut it — three equal parts.

64. He is acquitted — all blame.

65. The Pope absolved him — his oath of allegiance.

66. This fact does not accord — her declaration.

67. I do not agree — you; therefore I cannot agree — your proposal.

68. The queen bestowed — Tennyson the title of baron.

69. The college has conferred — my uncle the degree of Doctor of Divinity.

70. The two emperors conferred — each other for an hour.

71. He is conversant — many languages.

72. They were independent — each other.

73. His sisters are dependent — him.

74. That is not derogatory — their character.

75. I dissent — that proposition.

76. We are glad — his promotion.

77. He has a taste — poetry; she, a thirst — knowledge.

78. In 1842 he emerged — obscurity.

79. His property was merged — the common stock.

80. She often went — town shopping.

81. He plunged — the deepest part of the lake.

82. These bands of Indians were accompanied — settlers from Detroit.

83. The settlers were in company — Indians.

84. His proposal is likely to stir up ill-will — the various classes.

85. The Greeks, fearing that they would be surrounded, wheeled about and halted, with the river — their backs.

86. We are within three miles — Salisbury.

Omitted Prepositions.[1]—"Beware of omitting a preposition that is needed to make the meaning clear or the sentence grammatical."[2]

"Before 'home' the preposition 'at' should never be omitted, but the preposition 'to' is always omitted: *e. g.*, 'I am going home.'"[1]

EXERCISE LXXXIV.

Insert the necessary prepositions in the following sentences:—

1. What use is this piece of ribbon?
2. The oak was five feet diameter.
3. My business prevented me attending the last meeting of the committee.
4. I could not refrain shedding tears.
5. The remark is worthy the fool that made it.
6. It is unworthy your notice.
7. He lives the other side the river.
8. He fled the country, and went either to England or France.
9. Ignorance is the mother of fear as well as admiration.
10. Religion is a comfort in youth as well as old age.
11. It's no use to give up.
12. This side the mountain the country is thickly settled: the other side there are few inhabitants.
13. I wrote Mr. Knapp to come Wednesday, and promised that he should find us home.
14. Wealth is more conducive to worldliness than piety.
15. He is not home, but I think he is coming home to-night.

Redundant Prepositions.[1]—Beware of inserting prepositions which are not needed.

EXERCISE LXXXV.

Strike out the redundant prepositions:—

1. He met a boy of about eighteen years old.
2. Cadmus stood pondering upon what he should do.
3. Let a gallows be erected of fifty cubits high.
4. Hercules was very willing to take the world off from his shoulders and give it to Atlas again.

---

[1] "Foundations," p. 149.   [2] Ibid., p. 150.

5. No one can help from loving her.

6. From thence in two days the Greeks marched twenty miles.

7. There was much of wisdom in their plan.

8. A workman fell off of the ladder.

9. On one day I caught five trout, on another twelve.

10. We must examine into this subject more carefully.

11. A child copies after its parents.

12. The proposal to go to the woods was approved of by all of the boys.

13. At about what time will father return ?

14. After having heard his story, I gave him a dollar.

15. The spring is near to the house.

16. Bruno followed on after his master.

17. Wanted, a young man of from sixteen to twenty-one years of age.

18. They went on to the steamer soon after dinner.

19. Look out of the window.

CHAPTER VIII.

OF CONJUNCTIONS

Vulgarisms.[1]—Every educated person is expected to know the correct use of the following words:—

Like, as.—In good use *like* is never a conjunction, and therefore it cannot be used instead of *as* to introduce a clause. It is incorrect to say, "Walk *like* I walk;" but one may say, "He walks *like* me," or "He looks *like* his grandfather."[2]

Except, without, unless.—*Except*, which was originally a past-participle, was once in good use as a conjunction; but in modern use it has been displaced as a conjunction by *unless*, and is now a preposition only. We may say, "All went *except* me," but we may not say, "*Except* you go with me, I will stay at home." Another word not in good use as a conjunction, but often heard instead of "unless," is *without*.

EXERCISE LXXXVI.

Insert the proper word in each blank:—

Like, as.

1. Do — I do.
2. She fears a chicken — you fear a snake.
3. Thin bushy hair falls down on each side of his face somewhat — Longfellow's hair did in his later life.
4. I wish I could sing — she can.
5. I will be a lawyer — my father.
6. I will be a lawyer — my father was.
7. She looks — (if) she were crying.
8. He acted — (if) he were guilty.
9. Our snow-tunnel looked — we imagined Aladdin's cave looked.
10. He treated me — a cat treats a mouse.
11. Seventy-five cents a day will not feed those men — they wish to be fed.

---

[1] "Foundations," p. 152.   [2] See page 109.

12. The lines in this stanza are not forced — in other stanzas.

13. If I were a boy — Ralph is, I would try to stop the thing.

Except, without, unless.

14. I do not know how my horse got away — somebody untied him.

15. Do not come — you hear from me.

16. I will not go — father is willing.

17. I will not go — father's consent.

18. — you study better, you will be dropped.

19. It will be cool to-morrow — a hot wave comes.

20. I cannot go — money.

21. I cannot go — father sends me some money.

22. I will be there promptly — I hear from you.

23. Do not write — you feel in the mood for it.

24. She has no fault — diffidence.

25. She has no fault — it be diffidence.

26. He cannot enlist — with his guardian's consent.

Misused Conjunctions.[1]—Conjunctions are few in number and are more definite in their meanings than prepositions. Most errors in using them spring from confused thinking or hasty writing. "A close reasoner and a good writer in general may be known by his pertinent use of connectives."[2]

And.—*And* has, generally speaking, the meaning of "in addition to."

But.—*But* implies some exception, opposition, or contrast. Equivalent, or nearly equivalent, expressions are "however," "on the other hand," "yet,", "nevertheless."

As.—"*As* has so many meanings that it is better, when possible, to use a conjunction that covers less ground."[3]

Because, for, since.—The difference between these words is chiefly a difference in emphasis. "We will not go, *because* it is raining" is the strongest way of expressing the relation of cause and effect. In "*Since* it is raining, we will not go," the emphasis is shifted from

---

[1] "Foundations," p. 152.
[2] Coleridge: Table Talk. Quoted by A. S. Hill in Principles of Rhetoric.
[3] "Foundations," p. 153.

the cause to the effect, which becomes the prominent idea. In " We will not go, *for* it is raining," the reason, " it is raining," is announced as itself a bit of news. Often the choice between these words is decided by the ear.

How.—*How* properly means "in what manner" or "to what extent." It is often misused for " that" to introduce an object clause.

Nor, or.—*Nor* is the correlative of *neither*, sometimes of other negatives. *Or* is the correlative of *either*.

Therefore, so.—In the sense of "for this reason," *therefore* is preferable to *so*, since *so* has other meanings.

Though.—*Though* means "notwithstanding," "in spite of the fact that."

As if, as though.—"*As if* is, on the whole, preferable to *as though*."[1]

When, while.—*When* means "at the time that ;" *while*, "during the time that," "as long as." "*When* fixes attention on a date or period ; *while* fixes attention on the lapse of time."[2]

EXERCISE LXXXVII.

Insert the proper conjunction in each blank, if a conjunction is needed. Do not confine your choice to those mentioned above :—

1. Roland was mild and modest, — Charles was coarse and boastful.

2. — they were without provisions, they thought they should starve.

3. In Addison's day innumerable vices were prevalent, — chief among them was the custom of drinking.

4. Charles was a large, brawny fellow, — Orlando was a slender youth.

5. When the barn was full of people, the doors were suddenly shut and bolted — the barn was set on fire.

6. Hereward's men wanted booty, — Hereward took them to the Golden Borough.

7. He read a short — interesting account of "Theobald's."

8. Longfellow received a good education — he was not a poor boy.

9. He was disappointed in the speed of his yacht, — he had expected her to be very fast.

10. The man said "to sell" was not needed on the sign — no one would expect the hats to be given away.

[1] " Foundations," p. 156.   [2] Ibid., p. 157.

11. There is no doubt — the earth is spherical.

12. I know very little about the "Arabian Nights" — I have never read that book.

13. When Gulliver began to pull, the ships would not move — their anchors held them.

14. He had to be cautious in using his Bible — at that time reading it was prohibited ; — he fastened it with tapes on the underside of a stool.

15. The Liberal Arts Building at Chicago had twice as much iron in its frame — the Brooklyn Bridge.

16. The lumbermen must keep open a road to the railroad, — all their provisions must be brought from the city.

17. Scarcely had I thrown in my line — I felt a nibble.

18. The fly seems to have been created for no other purpose — to purify the air.

19. At first you wonder where the boats are, — on entering the grove you can see only a small cabin.

20. I do not doubt — he will succeed.

21. I cannot deny — he is honest.

22. He was dismissed, not so much because he was too young — because he was indolent.

23. The land is equally adapted to farming — to pasturage.

24. Proportion is — simple — compound.

25. I wonder — he will come.

26. The last of the horses had scarcely crossed the bridge — the head of the third battalion appeared on the other side.

27. He looked as — he could play football.

28. — I saw her, she was young — beautiful.

29. Bruce spoke of himself as being neither Scotch — English.

30. I could — buy — borrow it.

31. He has no love — veneration for his superiors.

32. There was no place so hidden — so remote — the plague did not find it.

33. We need not, — do not, complain of our lot.

34. He could not deny — he had borrowed money.

35. There is no question — the universe has bounds.

36. A corrupt government is nothing else — a reigning sin.

37. She thinks, I regret to say, of little else — clothes.

38. O fairest flower, no sooner blown — blasted.

39. There is no other hat here — mine.

7

40. — you have come, I will go with you.
41. — Virgil was the better artist, Homer was the greater genius.
42. He has not decided — he will let me go to college.
43. Sheep are white — black.
44. The King has no arbitrary power; your Lordships have not; — the Commons; — the whole Legislature.
45. No tie of gratitude — of honor could bind him.
46. She had no sooner arrived — she prepared to go boating.
47. Scarcely had she left the house — she returned.
48. He was punished, — he was guilty.
49. He was punished, — he was not guilty.
50. We cannot go — we finish our task.
51. — the rain came down in torrents, we started for the lake.
52. She could — dance — sing, — she played the piano.
53. I do not know — I shall walk — ride.
54. Hardly had he left the room — the prisoner attempted to escape.
55. The chances are ten to one — he will forget it.
56. Stand up so — you can be seen.

Omitted Conjunctions.—Careless writers sometimes omit conjunctions that are necessary either to the grammar or to the sense. A common form of this fault is illustrated in "This is as good if not better than that"—a sentence in which "as" is omitted after "as good." The best way to correct the sentence is to recast it, thus: "This is as good as that, if not better."

EXERCISE LXXXVIII.

Correct the faults in these sentences:—
1. Ralph is as young or younger than Harry.
2. Cedar is more durable but not so hard as oak.
3. I never heard any one speak more fluently or so wittily as he.
4. She is fairer but not so amiable as her sister.
5. Though not so old, he is wiser than his brother.

Redundant Conjunctions.[1]—Careless writers sometimes insert conjunctions that are useless or worse than useless.

[1] See "Foundations," pp. 208–211.

A common form of this fault is the use in certain cases of "and" or "but" before the words "who," "which," "when," or "where," which are themselves connectives: as, "The challenge was accepted by Orlando, a young man little known up to that time, *but* to *whom* Rosalind had taken a great liking." If the relative clause introduced by "who," "which," "when," or "where" is to be joined to a preceding relative clause, the conjunction is proper: as, "The challenge was accepted by Orlando, a young man *who* was little known at that time, *but* to whom Rosalind had taken a great liking."

EXERCISE LXXXIX.

Which conjunctions in these sentences are redundant?—

1. I have again been so fortunate as to obtain the assistance of Dr. Jones, a teacher of great experience, and whose ideas are quite in harmony with my own.

2. Franklin had noticed for some time the extreme dirtiness of the streets, and especially of the street that he lived on.

3. This animal was considered as irresistible.

4. But how to get him there was a problem. But it was decided to convey him on one of the wagons used in carrying the Emperor's men-of-war from the woods, where they were made, to the water.

5. He forgot to pay for the wine—a shortness of memory common with such men, and which his host did not presume to correct.

6. Next came Louis, Duke of Orleans, the first prince of the blood royal, and to whom the attendants rendered homage as the future king.

7. So from all this you can see that such things are not impossible.

8. Her expression of countenance induced most persons to address her with a deference inconsistent with her station, and which nevertheless she received with easy composure.

9. Our escort consisted of MacGregor, and five or six of the handsomest, best armed, and most athletic mountaineers of his band, and whom he had generally in immediate attendance upon his own person.

10. The little town of Lambtos, Mrs. Gardiner's former home, and where she had lately learned that some acquaintance still remained.

11. He spoke in a deep and low tone, but which nevertheless was heard from one end of the hall to the other.

Misplaced Correlatives.—When conjunctions are used as correlatives, as "both–and," "either–or," each of the correlated words should be so placed as to indicate clearly what ideas are to be connected in thought. This principle is violated in "He *not only* visited Paris, *but* Berlin *also*." In this sentence the position of "not only" before the verb "visited" leads one to expect some corresponding verb in the second part of the sentence; in fact, however, the two connected words are "Paris" and "Berlin;" "visited" applies to both. This meaning is clearly indicated by putting "not only" before "Paris:" thus, "He visited *not only* Paris, *but* Berlin *also*." As a rule the word after the first correlative should be the same part of speech as the word after the second correlative.

EXERCISE XC.

Correct the errors of position in—

1. Few complaints were made either by the men or the women.

2. Search-lights are not useful only on ships, but also on land.

3. Adversity both teaches to think and to be patient.

4. My uncle gave me not only the boat, but also taught me to row it.

5. The prisoner was not only accused of robbery, but of treason.

6. The wise ruler does not aim at the punishment of offenders, but at the prevention of offences.

7. The king was weak both in body and mind.

8. He either is stupid or insolent.

9. He worked not to provide for the future, but the present.

10. Every composition is liable to criticism both in regard to its design and to its execution.

11. The gods are either angry or nature is too powerful.

12. We are neither acquainted with the Doctor nor with his family.

13. In estimating the work of Luther, we must neither forget the temper of the man nor the age in which he lived.

14. The wise teacher should not aim to repress, but to encourage his pupils.

15. Such rules are useless both for teachers and pupils.

16. Her success is neither the result of cleverness nor of studiousness.

APPENDIX

SUGGESTIONS TO TEACHERS

THE following suggestions are made in answer to many inquiries from teachers who perceive the rare excellence of the "Foundations of Rhetoric," but who do not clearly see, because of the novel method of the book, how to turn its merits to account in their class-rooms. The suggestions outline one way in which the book has been used to great advantage.

It should never be forgotten that the illustrative sentences in the "Foundations" have no value except as they help the student to grasp a principle that he can apply in his own use of language. In every case the emphasis should be laid on the principle which is announced or illustrated. Merely learning the corrected sentences by heart is useless and should not be permitted.

In taking a class over PART I., which treats of words, it is the writer's practice to assign a short lesson — from one to three pages — in connection with every recitation in English. The leading ideas and most typical sentences in each lesson are privately marked in the teacher's book with colored pencil, so that they may readily catch his eye, and from five to twelve minutes of each recitation period are taken up with a rapid questioning on these leading ideas and typical sentences. Corrections or answers unaccompanied by reasons are not accepted. Attention is always fixed, not on the form of the illustrative sentence, but on the principle of usage under discussion. Pupils would rather commit to memory the sentences than trouble themselves about reasons; but they will master reasons when they find they must. After principles have been mastered, exercises in the choice of forms and words are needed in order that knowledge may be converted into habit.

In PARTS II. and III. the lessons are equally short and the emphasis is unceasingly laid on the question "Why?" If the subject is difficult, it is desirable, at the time that the lesson is assigned, to lead the class over the text and some of the illustrative sentences in order to open, as it were, the eyes of the pupils. Since these parts of the book treat not of single words, but of sentences and paragraphs, recitations on them seem to call for the use of pencil or chalk. One successful teacher conducts the recitation with books open, requiring her pupils to cover the correct sentences with a strip of paper while they explain and correct the faults in the incorrect sentences. The writer's practice is to paste the faulty sentences on cards of convenient size and thickness—the arrangement of columns is such that the sentences can all be cut from *one* old book—and to distribute them among eight or ten pupils at the beginning of the recitation hour. While other matters are being attended to, these pupils write the sentences in correct form on the blackboard, and, when the time comes, give their reasons for the changes which they have made. Their work is discussed, if necessary, by the whole class. Reviews and written tests should be frequent. As fast as the various principles explained and illustrated in PARTS II. and III. are studied, the attention of pupils should be immediately turned to their own writing. It will be far more profitable for them to correct their own offences against clearness, force, ease, and unity than to correct similar offences committed by others. For this reason the PRACTICAL EXERCISES IN ENGLISH contains no exercises on the subjects discussed in PARTS II. and III. of the "Foundations."

CPSIA information can be obtained at www.ICGtesting.com
Printed in the USA
LVOW071055110313

323657LV00007B/159/A